D0205501

"*Inside the Red Zone* offers no excuses for the pain brought about by Saddam Hussein, but unlike the mainstream media, Ferner's book lifts up the rubble to show us the casualties of the war—mothers and children—and the costs of a conflict far from over."

Michael Sallah
Investigations Editor for the *Miami Herald*

"There exists in America today a well-publicized illusion, manufactured by Washington, that we are somehow in Iraq to wage war against Islamic terrorists, "Islamofascists" and formless evil. Ferner bursts through this flaßg-draped political façade, presenting what we are really doing in Iraq, to whom we are doing it, and what it is doing to us."

Karen Kwiatkowski, Ph.D., USAF Lt. Col. (ret.)
Retired early from her final assignment as a Political Military
Staff Officer in the Pentagon to write about the administration's
lies prior to the Iraq invasion in March 2003. She teaches in the
Political Science department at James Madison University.

"Secretary Colin Powell famously declared about civilian casualties in Iraq: 'It's really not a number I'm interested in.' Mike Ferner, a Veteran For Peace, has a passionate concern about the people of Iraq. *Inside the Red Zone* enables those of us who, like him, do care about the people of Iraq to gain some sense of the human cost of this war for those whose land happens to be over the huge oil deposits we have determined are of vital interest to us. Those who read this book will begin to share Mike Ferner's deeply felt determination to end this war as quickly as possible."

Bishop Thomas J. Gumbleton
Archdiocese of Detroit

"Americans oppose the war on Iraq in large numbers because they understand that it was based on lies. Anyone who reads Mike Ferner's account of the people in Iraq whose lives are being destroyed will change the way they talk about this war. They will call it wrong, criminal, something that could never have been done the right way, no matter how competently performed. If they learned what is in this book they would not simply oppose the war by telling pollsters they oppose it. They would do what some of the most courageous and principled among us are doing. They would follow Mike Ferner's example and put their own safety and liberty on the line repeatedly to end the killing. Ferner has told the stories that can change minds and sets the example that needs to be followed."

David Swanson
Co-Founder, AfterDowningStreet.org

INSIDE THE RED ZONE

A Veteran For Peace Reports from Iraq

MIKE FERNER

Foreword by Cindy Sheehan

PRAEGER

Westport, Connecticut
London

Library of Congress Cataloging-in-Publication Data

Ferner, Mike.
  Inside the Red Zone: a veteran for peace reports from Iraq / Mike Ferner ; foreword by
Cindy Sheehan.
    p. cm.
  Includes bibliographical references and index.
  ISBN 0–275–99243–8 (alk. paper)
  1. Iraq War, 2003—Protest movements—United States. 2. Pacifists—United States.
3. Iraq—Description and travel. I. Title.
DS79.76.F46   2006
956.7044′3—dc22   2006020992

British Library Cataloguing in Publication Data is available.

Library of Congress Catalog Card Number: 2006020992
ISBN: 0–275–99243–8

First published in 2006

Praeger Publishers, 88 Post Road West, Westport, CT 06881
An imprint of Greenwood Publishing Group, Inc.
www.praeger.com

Printed in the United States of America

The paper used in this book complies with the
Permanent Paper Standard issued by the National
Information Standards Organization (Z39.48-1984).

10 9 8 7 6 5 4 3 2 1

To the common heroes in the peace movement who tried to stop this war before it began; to the people of Iraq, from whom we have much to learn about being compassionate and humane despite the hellish conditions we have created in their land; to the veterans of this war who will not come home and those who come back committed to telling the truth about what their government sent them to do.

CONTENTS

PART III: ACTIVISTS, JOURNALISTS, SOLDIERS, AND CLOWNS

FOREWORD

Inside the Red Zone: A Veteran For Peace Reports from Iraq is an immensely important book in this day and age of news suppression from Iraq!

My friend, Mike Ferner, had the stunning courage to go to Iraq before the immoral and illegal invasion in 2003 and meet the people that our government was about to attack. Mike knew that the people that George Bush and company were demonizing were really just people, and he wanted to go and see for himself.

Now with, as some estimates say, at least 100,000 innocent Iraqis killed and the country lying in shambles, one might say that such an incredibly important book may be coming out too late, but I don't believe that. It may be too late for the poor unfortunates of Iraq and for American troops like my son, Casey, but it is not too late for the people still in harm's way.

At the moment that I write this, the leaders of our country are banging the war drums for an invasion of Iran. This would be a disaster and I hope while you are reading this that you are breathing a sigh of relief that it hasn't happened yet. But if the invasion doesn't happen, you can thank peace activists like Mike Ferner for their courage and conviction.

Inside the Red Zone gives us a very rare look into the average life of an Iraqi person pre- and post-invasion. Except for a few documentaries and stories on the Internet, I can't think of any mainstream journalist who has actually gone out among the people of the country. I remember stories of journalists riding in armored vehicles in the invasion wearing their body armor and showing the glory of our military might, but I don't remember one story of how this invasion was affecting the people of Iraq. It just wasn't done. The media have done a terrible job of putting a human face on this war.

In this age of comfort and consumerism above all else, Mike's book is important in telling the story of ordinary Americans who left the comfort and relative safety of America to save other members of humanity.

My entire mission, aside from calling for the immediate and complete withdrawal of the troops from Iraq, is to rally our fellow Americans to go out of their comfort zones to make the world a better place and it gives me so much pleasure and encouragement to read stories of Americans who went above and beyond the call of duty to put a human face on tragedy and to try and prevent it from happening. This book is an important tool for this work.

I am called Mother Courage in Europe and Latin American countries, and people always tell me how brave they think that I am. I am not brave. I do not fear anything. The people who are truly brave are the Mike Ferners of the world and the Kathy Kelleys and the Casey Sheehans.

To put one's life on the line for friends as Casey did is remarkable, but to go and do it for strangers and people you most likely will never meet is sacred. The world needs more heroes and far fewer cowards. The cowards send us to war, the heroes try to prevent needless killing.

I hope you, the reader, enjoy this book for what it is, a great adventure story, but more importantly, a call to action.

This book is a call for us, in any walk of life, to rejoin our humanity and the humanity of the world to put our lives on the line for peace with justice.

We will never have true and lasting peace in our world until the day that we forbid our leaders to demonize and marginalize other fellow human beings.

Mike Ferner gets this and I hope the world gets it too, before it is too late.

—Cindy Sheehan, January 2006

PREFACE

That you're holding this volume in your hand is proof that unexpected good luck still exists.

When I decided to go to Iraq in January 2004 with the intention to write, it was not just that I suspected corporate news outlets were leaving the U.S. public in the dark about some very important stories. It was because I had seen it for myself, multiple times, during my first trip there just prior to the U.S. invasion of March, 2003. So when I went back for two months early in 2004, it didn't take me long to find some of those stories. As you'll see from the instance at the courthouse in Ramadi, so many people had so many compelling stories you could literally get swept away.

But as I've heard it said, that unless you're Emily Dickinson, if you want to be a writer you need readers. Luckily the internet provides an outlet, albeit unpaid, for writers with something to say. Thanks to sites like Counterpunch, the Baltimore Chronicle, MRZine, Antiwar.com, truthout.org, selves and others, and LewRockwell.com, my work found responsive readers and I was encouraged to keep writing.

Another bit of good fortune was that in Iraq I met Dahr Jamail, now probably the most influential independent journalist covering that country, just as he began his work. Although I'll not likely attain his level of skill and certainly not his prodigious output, I did learn from him not to be discouraged by lack of a hardcopy portfolio or compensation, and just "get it out there" on the internet.

After many electronic articles and responses, the unprecedented thought struck me to compile these stories in a book. Because Hilary Claggett at Praeger Publishers believed they deserve to be told, you are holding *Inside the Red Zone: A Veteran For Peace Reports from Iraq.*

In these pages you'll meet some of the people who've inspired me to continue working in the peace movement and to become an author. Two deserve special mention.

The first is my wife, Sue Carter, who thinks I'm brave but is in reality the courageous one of us—not only for being an unfailing peace activist but for staring down a timeclock every morning, allowing her late middle-aged spouse to discover the work he truly loves.

The second is not really a single person but 24 million of them—the people of Iraq. Whatever success this book has will be measured by the extent to which readers begin to see them as fellow human beings.

INTRODUCTION

Through the summer of 2002 demands for war emanated from the White House and rolled across the land. That fall, they grew to a deafening roar as the administration of George W. Bush prepared the nation to invade Iraq. Still, the hearts of many beat a hopeful response that Bush's "preemptive" war would instead be a prevented war.

In retrospect, it might seem crazy to believe that ordinary people could keep the dogs of war leashed, but we truly did. And around the world millions more believed the same.

British rail workers began refusing to move war cargo. Italian unions called on members to lay down their tools in protest. In thousands of cities and small towns across the U.S., people marched and prayed. For once, a war faced global opposition before it began, never more clearly demonstrated than on February 15, 2003. On that single day, beginning in New Zealand and Australia, and sweeping westward across Japan, China, Indonesia, India, Russia, the Middle East, Africa, Europe, North and South America, over 10,000,000 people took to the streets to demand peace.

In those months before the invasion, hopes for peace also grew in Toledo, Ohio, a city of 300,000 on the western edge of Lake Erie. Along with hope, some of us also felt rising anger, frustration and resolve; vowing that this time, we would do more than hold a sign or attend a rally.

It was in this atmosphere that I concluded to do something that seemed more commensurate with the threat of war—to go to Iraq. I wasn't sure exactly why, or even what I would do when I got there. But I was compelled to do something more and going to Iraq made sense. A friend referred me to an organization that in the course of seven years had sent over 70 delegations of U.S. citizens to Iraq to learn how U.N. sanctions were affecting its people, then return home and speak about what they saw. As invasion looked more likely, Voices in the Wilderness shifted their focus from sanctions to trying to prevent a war, renaming its delegations Iraq Peace Teams (IPT).

By the time I heard of their work and applied to join a delegation, it was early January 2003, a little more than two months before 130,000 U.S. and British troops stormed out of Kuwait into Iraq. When friends and reporters in Toledo asked me what I would do in Iraq I replied that I was prepared to use my training as a Navy hospital corpsman to assist civilian casualties in case of war. Still hoping that would ultimately not be needed, I booked a flight and prepared to go.

As the days ticked by preceding my trip, word got around town. Local TV stations sent reporters to the house and right-wing radio talk show hosts had a field day. Voices in the Wilderness delegates routinely took boxes of medical supplies to Iraq in order to purposely violate the sanctions and make a political point, and people responded so enthusiastically to my request for over-the-counter medications that I added two more suitcases of these supplies to my luggage. One disturbed fellow phoned the house and recorded a death threat, claiming he was taking collections for a body bag, and hoped his son, then stationed in Kuwait, would run into me "after he kicks Saddam Hussein's ass."

After a stint in local politics, I had developed a pretty thick skin, and none of the negative comments bothered me very much. But the night before I left, lying in bed with my wife, thinking of how many U.S. and Iraqi soldiers were experiencing a similar "last night at home," the phone rang. A friend called to tell us that a local TV station had run one of those unscientific call-in "polls," asking the question: "Is Mike Ferner a traitor for going to Iraq?" A full 74% of my fellow citizens responding felt I should swing from the nearest yardarm.

My response was a crude admonition and a few deleted expletives. My wife, however, took the news to heart and in a moment was on the phone to the station's newsroom, telling them, "How dare you accuse my husband of being a traitor? He served four years on city council. He served in the military. And thanks to you, our lives may be in jeopardy." She later told me of receiving about a dozen hate calls and emails the first few days after I left, but those were eventually replaced by a far larger number of positive comments.

The Northwest Ohio Peace Coalition decided to hold a news conference on Saturday, February 1, the morning I left for the Middle East. As an indication of popular opposition to the war and how it would be covered by the news media, over 200 supporters came out for the news conference – and one local TV station.

That morning, people brought bags of medicines and supplies for me to take to Iraq, and pressed small donations into my hand as they said goodbye. One person I'd never met before introduced himself and wished me well.

He said, "This trip will change your life." I had no idea how true those words would become.

Inside the Red zone: A veteran for peace Reports from Irag takes its name from the unofficial term for that part of Baghdad, and by extension, all of Iraq, that lies outside the "Green Zone," a heavily fortified area on the Tigris River that used to be home to Saddam Hussein and his elites, now headquarters for the U.S. operations in Iraq. One day at breakfast in the Agadir Hotel, Dan Pepper, a photographer, sat down to tell us the morning's best story—an incident from the previous day when he was working in the Green Zone and ran into two Bechtel Corp. contractors. "They asked me where I lived in Baghdad, and when I told them a hotel on the other side of the Tigris, they asked excitedly, 'You mean you live in the Red Zone? Could you take some pictures for us so we can see what it looks like?"

Reading this modest volume will not provide you with the definitive political analysis of Iraq. But no one should be as ignorant about the lives of ordinary Iraqis as those Bechtel contractors. This book tells the story of a month I spent in Iraq just before the U.S. invasion as a member of a delegation of peace activists, and the two months I spent there a year later, as an independent journalist to write stories about ordinary people and how the war changed their lives . . . and mine.

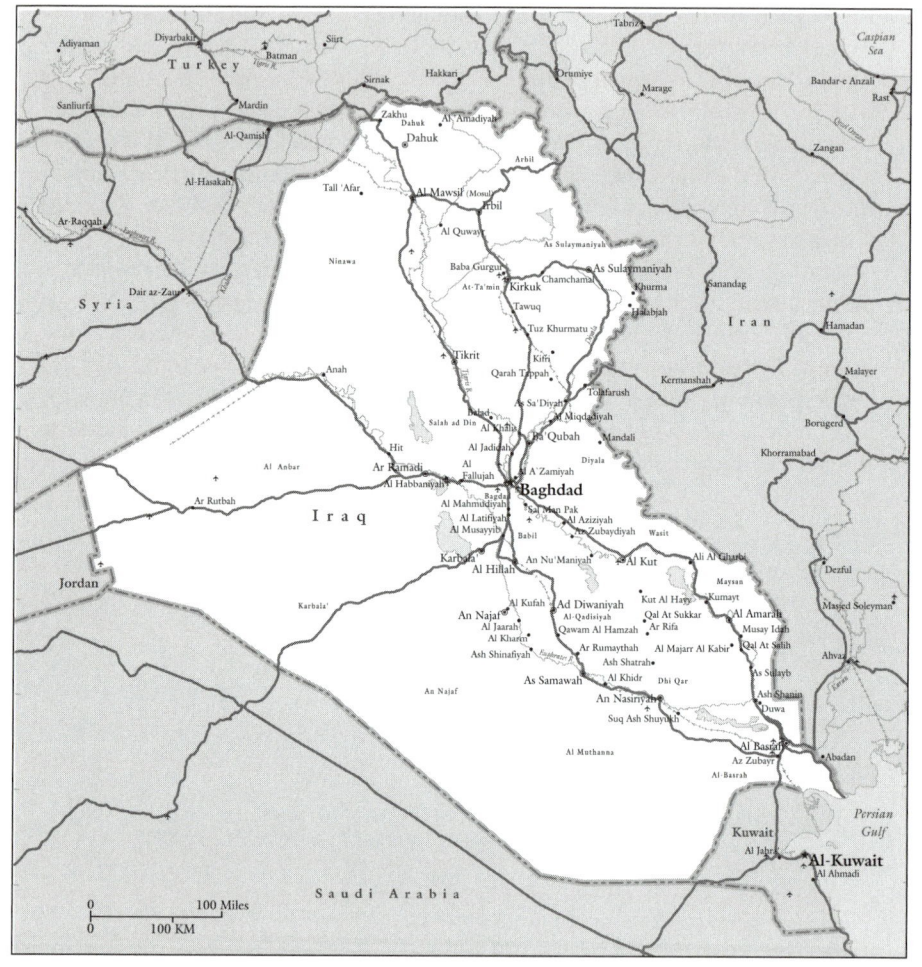

Map of Iraq.

PART I

WAITING FOR THE SKIES
TO RAIN MISSILES

1

INTO IRAQ

The flight to Jordan via Frankfurt took me farther abroad than I'd ever been. Delegations from Voices in the Wilderness (Voices) and later, their Iraq Peace Teams (IPTs), routinely gathered in Amman, lodging at a modest hotel less than a block down the street from a hotel coincidentally named the Toledo. Arriving a day early, I met a delegation from Christian Peacemaker Teams (CPT) also on their way to Baghdad, and this included Cliff Kindy, a farmer who lived less than 100 miles from me in the neighboring state of Indiana. We would see more of each other in Iraq.

My extra day in Amman allowed me to meet Ahab Said, a 28-year-old Palestinian living in Jordan who also worked in Yemen as a nurse and physical therapist. His primary focus, however, was a campaign to boycott U.S. products.

He was eager to explain what he said was a growing movement in the Arab world, admitting that the Jordanian government was opposed to it because it would affect the Jordanian economy as well, but he countered, "the people believe it might make a difference." He said part of what motivated support for the boycott was "when we support American companies we are also supporting Israel, because of the American taxes that go to Israel."

The boycott campaign began in September 2000, after Israeli Prime Minister Sharon visited the Al-Aqsa mosque in Jerusalem, Said continued, "because of the outrage in the Arab world caused by Sharon going to the mosque . . . and it grew greatly after September 11, 2001 when the U.S. attitude against the Arab world hardened."

Said explained that in Turkey and Lebanon, McDonald's Corporation's restaurants had been attacked by stone-throwing crowds. In Egypt, Coca-Cola Company officials had asked the courts to stop the spread of the boycott against their products. In Jordan, he claimed that many people, including a new group organized by doctors, attorneys, and other professionals, were boycotting Pepsi, Coke, and McDonald's Corporations, leading the Jordanian government to respond by declaring the boycott illegal and arresting some of the leaders.

A French Tunisian businessman had started producing Mecca Cola, which sold over two million cans in its first year, according to Said. About six months earlier, ZamZam Cola, an Iranian product, had joined Mecca Cola as an alternative to Western drinks. "The slogan we use is 'Think as a Muslim, drink as a Muslim,'" the Palestinian smiled.

"The boycott is in our hands, not in the government's hands," he continued, and claimed that it was spreading to other countries, such as Britain. He predicted the boycott would expand to include not only U.S. products but also events and speakers. "We will continue to welcome U.S. citizens, but U.S. government officials will not be welcome. All this will continue because of what Bush is doing to our people in Palestine and because it is an Islamic order."

The next day saw the arrival of Kathy Kelly, founder of Voices, and the rest of the IPT delegation on a flight from Chicago. Over dinner that night at the Toledo, we shared stories of our initial experiences in the peace movement. Lynn Macmichael got my immediate attention when she said her activism began in San Francisco during the Vietnam War, as part of an organization called the Carrier Project, a group that used nonviolent civil disobedience tactics to delay aircraft carriers setting sail for Vietnam. One of the carriers that she and a flotilla of small boats blockaded outside the Alameda Naval Air Station, in San Francisco Bay, was the USS *Hancock,* a ship I had served on during that period. Indeed, in late 1972, I worked at the air station's dispensary where our orders one day included "checking out some protesters the Coast Guard will drop off after they haul them out of the Bay." I can't swear that Lynn was one of those bedraggled, soggy protesters whose small craft had been swamped by the Coast Guard, but she might well have been.

The next leg of our journey, a thirteen-hour road trip to Baghdad, began in the predawn darkness of February 5, as our driver, Sattar, and his assistant helped us load our bags into two SUVs. He checked to make sure we had enough water with us, and waited for one straggler to take a final picture of the marquee of the Toledo Hotel. He explained that besides wanting to get an early start, it was important for him to leave Amman before 7:00 a.m. An ordinance was in force to protect local cabbies from out-of-town competitors during business hours. So it was that we were on the road between Haldi and Safawi as the sun rose over the flat, distant horizon.

Sattar had made the trip countless times and Voices delegations relied on him almost exclusively for transportation to Baghdad. He knew every turn in the road, every w.c. (bathroom) break, and every waiter at the lunch stop. A civil engineer by training, he kept his orange and white GMC in tip-top shape and fastidiously clean. Unable to find work in his chosen field, a problem he shared with many well-educated Iraqis, he took his driving job seriously and was devoted to his friends from Voices and CPT. Later, during the war, with the bombed hulks of Iraqi tanks littering the side of the road and shrapnel dotting the highway between Baghdad and Amman, he still drove peace activists in and out of the country.

Except for an occasional rolling hill, the landscape was flat and barren. The main difference visible at 70 mph was that in Jordan, black rocks ranging in size from a fist to a person's head covered the land almost completely. Closer to Iraq, the land flattened and the rocks nearly disappeared and we began to see shepherds and their flocks every few miles. What the sheep ate was almost impossible to tell. Short stretches of a barely perceptible, green fuzz of vegetation was all that interrupted what looked like otherwise barren earth.

Human habitation was equally sparse. Here was a tent dwelling, there a mud hut, sometimes set many hundreds of yards back from the four-lane highway. Every few miles, we passed a person standing alongside the road, looking for all the world like they were waiting at a bus stop, except there was nothing to mark it as such, and the lack of any buildings in the area made it seem as though they had been dropped onto a moonscape by extraterrestrials.

A hundred yards or more to the side of the highway was another roadway used solely by a steady procession of oil tankers carrying petroleum products from Iraq to Jordan. In the early '90s the Hussein government constructed a separate roadway for oil tankers. On our portion of the highway there were very few cars and almost no trucks of any sort.

Three things stood out on that memorable trip: the stark flatness of the landscape stretching to the horizon in all directions under a cloudless blue sky; stopping in a particularly remote area to listen to the deafening quiet; and the two hours of inspections and red tape it took to cross the border into Iraq—a crossing that would have undoubtedly taken longer without Sattar's expertise at crossing the right palms with a little silver.

Sattar selected me from the delegation to go with him around the far side of the customs house for an additional "inspection," which was the excuse for separating us from a couple of ten dollar bills. When Sattar held his finger to his lips, I easily imagined myself part of some deliciously dangerous international intrigue.

While I sat in the car behind the customs house and waited for Sattar, I saw a group of about fifteen Iraqi men, women, and children walk by, carrying bundles of household goods. "Are they getting out?" I wondered. I looked at their faces carefully as they walked by. It occurred to me that theirs could well be the faces of the "enemy" we could soon be slaughtering.

From the car window I saw a pigeon, the only one I'd seen so far on the trip, alight nearby. It was all white and resembled a dove. I took this as a good sign. Three young truck drivers exited the customs house, chatting pleasantly on their way back to their trucks, probably happy to be done with the red tape for this trip. "Towelheads," some Americans would call them. One looked remarkably like my friend, Brian Uram, back in Toledo, Ohio.

Back on the road, now in Iraq, Sattar talked more about life in his country.

He said that most men now worked more than one job. Most women stayed at home, but more worked outside the home now than before the 1991 war with the United States. The Iraqi currency, the dinar, prior to the war was worth $3.30. Now it took 2,200 dinars to buy one dollar, and that figure was rising rapidly. He also explained that although Americans consider the 1991 war against Iraq the "First Iraq War" and the looming one the Second, Iraqis call the Iran-Iraq War the First and the 1991 conflict the Second War.

I asked our engineer-turned-taxi driver more questions about life in Iraq: Were people going hungry? What was the healthcare system like? What about education?

"The basic foods like rice, sugar, tea, milk, and flour are included in the government's ration program," Sattar said. "Each month every family gets a regular amount. With war coming, the government is starting to double up the amounts. Last month people got December and January's rations, and this month they'll get February and March's. Before the First War, health care was free or cost very little to everyone in the country. Since then, it remains free or low-cost to children, the old and women, but not men . . . Before the Second War, school teachers were paid well and they tried hard to educate the children. But now, it is very difficult. There is not enough money to pay them well or for supplies. The education is not as good as it was when I was a student."

Hours later, cramped, exhausted, and excited, we arrived in Baghdad as dusk fell outside our new home-away-from-home, the Al-Fanar Hotel on Abu Nuwas Street.

As we slumped in lobby chairs, a parade of buses drove past filled with young people leaning out the windows, blowing trumpets, banging drums, waving, and singing. Ready to be suspicious of Saddam Hussein's Iraq, my first thought was, "Who do they think is going to fall for this hokey welcoming party business?" Exactly one week from the night we arrived, I learned the same thing happened every Thursday evening. On the night before the Islamic holy day of Friday, much like Saturday nights in the west, it's common for young people to get married. Just down the street from the Fanar was a popular park for wedding ceremonies, and across a narrow side street were the Palestine and the Sheraton Hotels, both hot spots for parties and receptions. So it really *wasn't* all about us . . . ?

With that realization came another: The people in this city of four million, whose water, sewer, electric, and phone installations were smashed by U.S. bombings in the 1991 war, and who were deprived of many necessities by the intervening years of harsh sanctions, lived each day expecting the skies to open up and rain cruise missiles on their heads at any moment. Yet they not only carried on with what appeared to be remarkably normal lives, they did so with hope for the future, proven by continuing to get married and starting families.

♦ ♦ ♦

I wrote this just before I left for Iraq. It was published as a commentary on February 4, 2003 in the Toledo Blade.

WHY I'M GOING TO IRAQ

On February 3, along with a dozen other U.S. citizens, I'll arrive in Baghdad to live for a month as part of a delegation organized by the Iraq Peace Team.

I'm going because as a 19-year-old Navy corpsman I nursed the blind, crippled, and insane young men sacrificed by the Nixon administration in Viet Nam. And now I see the unelected Bush administration preparing to kill its youth and rain death on millions of innocent Iraqis for the most corrupt reasons imaginable—to expand the American empire and help U.S. companies dominate the world's resources.

I'm going because I need to do something more than carry a sign; something commensurate with the horrors about to unfold. I want people in Iraq to know that we Americans are not as reckless and insane as our leaders. And if necessary, I want to use the skills my government taught me 30 years ago as a cog in the war machine, to assist innocent Iraqi victims of war.

My decision is neither brave nor heroic, simply what I must do. I don't believe any of us common folk can prevent a war by going to Iraq because our government does not treasure the lives of common folk. It treasures property. If that were not so, we would have universal health care and safe, efficient mass transit. We would provide for our aged and children before comforting the privileged.

Our president doesn't care if common Americans are safe in their own country, and neither will he care about our safety in Iraq—unless we make him care. I believe we can make him care and stop this war, if we each do what we must. For example:

- In Britain recently, two railroad engineers refused to move a train carrying ammunition for the war.
- Around the world thousands of people are peacefully committing civil disobedience, thereby practicing the highest form of citizenship. As Thoreau put it, they are not just casting a paper ballot, but "clog with their whole weight" as they protest injustice.
- Active-duty troops and reservists can heed this "Call to Conscience" issued by U.S. veterans: "If the people of the world are ever to be free, there must come a time when being a citizen of the world takes precedence over being the soldier of a nation. Now is that time. When your orders come to ship out . . . your response will help set the course of our future . . . Your commanders want you to obey. We urge you to think . . . to (use) your conscience. If you choose to

resist, we will support you and stand with you because we have come to understand that our REAL duty is to the people of the world and to our common future."

- Our troops can consider the words of Marine Corps General Smedley Butler, who exposed how the military serves the interests of property in the corporate form. This Medal-of-Honor winner wrote: " . . . I helped make Haiti and Cuba a decent place for the National City Bank boys to collect revenues in. I helped in the raping of half a dozen Central American republics for the benefit of Wall Street . . . In China in 1927 I helped see to it that Standard Oil went its way unmolested." Butler acknowledged that he'd spent most of his 33 years in the Marines as "a high class muscle man for . . . Wall Street . . . I was a racketeer, a gangster for capitalism."

- We can warm our hearts with words spoken by a truly heroic American, Eugene Debs. Five months before World War One ended, he gave his famous Canton, Ohio Speech, for which he received a federal prison sentence. He said in part: "Wars throughout history have been waged for conquest and plunder. In the Middle Ages when the feudal lords . . . concluded to enlarge their domains . . . they declared war upon one another. But they themselves did not go to war any more than the modern feudal lords, the barons of Wall Street go to war . . . the working class who fight all the battles . . . and furnish the corpses, have never yet had a voice in either declaring war or making peace. If war is right let it be declared by the people."

Today we are still governed by modern feudal lords who wish to enlarge their domains by sending us serfs to war. What will it take to become a self-governing nation—where the vast decency, wisdom, and compassion of the American people finally guide our foreign and domestic policies?

More and more I'm convinced people like historian Howard Zinn know what it will take. He wrote: "Civil disobedience is not our problem. Our problem is civil obedience. Our problem is that people all over the world have obeyed the dictates of leaders . . . and millions have been killed because of this obedience . . . Our problem is that people are obedient all over the world in the face of poverty and starvation and stupidity, and war, and cruelty. Our problem is that people are obedient while the jails are full of petty thieves . . . (and) the grand thieves are running the country."

I believe we will see a better day—but not until we withdraw our consent and cease being obedient in the face of poverty and war and cruelty. Our times demand more of us. The planet and all its species demand more of us. We must each do what we can . . . and do it now.

2

THE GUARDIANS OF REALITY DO THEIR THING

After a day of just getting used to the idea that I was in Baghdad, I learned that Bret Eartheart, the IPT delegate responsible for press relations, was going back home to Bloomington, Indiana. Having done this kind of work for citizens' groups in the United States for many years, my job in Iraq suddenly became clear.

My predecessor took me on a swing through the sprawling Ministry of Information, to introduce me to scores of reporters from every corner of the world. In the month he'd held this position for IPT, he had gotten to know journalists from Turkey, China, Japan, South Africa, Portugal, Brazil, Greece, England, Italy, Korea, France, Egypt, Spain and, of course, Iraq, and the United States. Inside the vast "press center," rows of glorified cubicles, looking like large shipping containers with doors, buzzed with a babel of languages and activity. My head spun as I took notes on this United Nations of journalism, trying to remember whom I was meeting from where.

Several reporters worked out of their hotels instead of the Ministry building, meaning that distributing a news release was not complete without visiting the Al-Mansour, the Al-Rashid, the Sheraton-Palestine complex, the Flowerland Hotel, and a couple of others. Some people claimed that in those days, no Westerners went anywhere in Baghdad without one of Saddam's agents on their tail. I made my news rounds day and night, and never noticed anyone following me. But if I was followed, the agent certainly earned his pay trying to follow my crazy, circuitous route through Baghdad, hopping in and out of cabs.

One highlight of the job was walking from the Ministry to the offices of Al-Jazeera News, to visit with the bureau chief if he was in. Getting to Al-Jazeera required a lengthy hike past vacant lots used by grazing donkeys and kids playing soccer, and down to the Tigris River for a short stroll, to a picturesquely crumbling, turquoise building. Two flights up were the offices of Al-Jazeera. Vilified by the Bush administration for "slanted" coverage, the

Al-Jazeera reporters were fond of describing the difference this way: "Your media covers the rockets taking off. We report from where they land." Very likely one of the reporters I said hello to in the hallways was the one killed a month later by a U.S. rocket when the Pentagon ordered the station blown off the air for its coverage of the bombing of Baghdad.

By day, I met with the leadership of the IPT contingent to plan activities, attend that day's event, write a release describing the next day's event, find a photocopy shop, and set out on another round of early-evening distributions.

If you find it hard to believe that such a simple-sounding agenda could easily take ten hours of focused energy, consider this. It's one thing to sit down at your computer in the United States, knock out a couple of pages, click "print," walk a few feet to the copy machine, hit "copy", and away you go. It's quite another to wait your turn at one of two laptops shared with twenty or more saintly but computer-challenged people trying to write emails home and copy them to a disk so they can run it across the street to one of the few internet stations in town, wait for the lone portable printer fouled with grit deposited by the last dust storm, and keep your fingers crossed when you hit "print." Once a printed news release was extracted from the quiet pandemonium of the IPT office, the next stop was for copies, where a typical transaction included sipping hot tea with the shop proprietor eager to tell me all about his uncle living in California since 1970, as the "Who" played over a tinny radio in the background.

On such a shoestring, with such passion and purpose, we joined with others around the globe trying to stop a war.

Our niche in the peace movement was that we were Westerners, in Iraq, telling our own governments not to make war on that nation. For example, on February 8 we dashed to the Baghdad airport to greet Hans Blix and the UN weapons inspectors as they returned to resume their duties. Our banners, displayed to get the attention of the international press corps said, "INSPECTIONS, YES. INVASION, NO!"

On that day, I sent the first of several reports back to friends, family, and press. In retrospect, its hopeful appeal seems all the more heartbreaking.

"We are planning a week of activities here in Baghdad and are counting on activists around the world to join with us in order to turn the tide. We can do it. We can stop a war against Iraq. We can make such a difference in the lives of people in this country. We can prevent a tidal wave of suffering and death. We can show that people around the globe can and will unite to demand the kind of life we deserve . . . What we do here, and more importantly, what YOU do where you live will make an enormous difference—literally a life-and-death difference. We are counting on you as never before."

During that week, we went to water treatment plants, electric plants, bridges, and hospitals in Baghdad, the sort of infrastructure targets Bush the Elder bombed in 1991, and hung banners that said in English and Arabic: "TO BOMB THIS SITE IS A VIOLATION OF THE GENEVA CONVENTIONS

Members of Voices in the Wilderness' Iraq Peace Team are joined by members of Christian Peacemaker Teams, at the Taji Electric Plant, Baghdad, February 2003. Just weeks before the U.S. "shock and awe" campaign and invasion, activists hung banners on electric generating stations, water treatment plants, hospitals, and bridges to caution George W. Bush against bombing civilian infrastructure like his father had done in the 1991 Gulf War. As indicated by the shadows in the foreground, many reporters turned out for these events, but during the month I was there, never any from U.S. news media outlets. (*Photo by Thorne Anderson*)

ARTICLE 94." Those events were planned to culminate on February 15, the day when millions of people throughout the world planned to demonstrate against a U.S. invasion.

My report home on February 11 began with a description of a 7:00 a.m. trip the previous morning to the UN compound on Canal Street, to greet the weapons inspectors beginning another shift in their high-profile jobs. One inspector dodged six lanes of speeding traffic to get to our side of the street and thank us for being there. "It boosts our morale," he said with a smile.

My report continued, "Then it was off to the al-Amariyah shelter, where over 400 people were killed by a cruise missile strike 12 years ago tomorrow. It is an overwhelmingly sad memorial. Basically a large, high-ceilinged, one-story building, it was built with triple-reinforced concrete roof and double-reinforced concrete walls. There's a gaping hole in the roof, with twisted re-bar rods where the missile entered and a small crater where it exploded. But when that happened, a fireball and concussion killed just about everyone in the shelter . . . a section of floor has been roped off that contains grisly 'shadows' made from human flesh seared into the concrete. I was in the shelter with another IPT member and a Spanish TV crew who wanted to do a segment on a veteran's perspective. After walking through the shelter I could hardly talk to the reporter. It was just overwhelming—and this after all the dead had long been removed. I'm told people now will not go into shelters because they're afraid they'll be targeted again, and clearly they're not up to keeping out a cruise missile. The Elder Bush administration, of course, said that it was an errant missile, that we would never target a shelter. But even if that's the truth, the people are just as dead. Could this incident have been where we first heard the term 'collateral damage?'"

My report home that day concluded, "Please take a look at the release below, (titled: 'PEACE ACTIVISTS POST BANNER ON POWER STATION, WARN BUSH AGAINST COMMITTING WAR CRIMES') about our action today at the electric plant. I hope people all over the country will join with us and hang banners at electric plants, water plants, bridges, etc., whether it's this week or next . . . the only thing that will stay the mad hand of Dubya is a massive rising of our fellow citizens, withdrawing their consent from the government, sitting down, throwing a wrench in the works of business as usual. The American people have a choice to act or not. The people of Iraq don't have that choice. They can only wait and hope."

Each time we hung a banner in Baghdad or issued a statement, we were nearly mobbed by the international press, but only once in the month I was there, when we held a news conference right at the Ministry of Information's press center, did a U.S. news outlet, CNN, show up. A U.S. network might rarely pick up something Reuters did on us, but that was the exception. The IPT delegates, by now numbering around forty-five from five countries, were astounded at how blatant the blackout was. Here is one example, from CBS News.

One evening as I passed out a news release and chatted with reporters in the Information Ministry I wore my Veterans For Peace cap. Hearing someone in an American accent hail me, I turned and was greeted by someone who introduced himself as an ex-Marine. We traded stories for a couple of minutes and then he told me he was a producer for CBS TV, in Baghdad for a few days to produce the "Early Show" with Harry Smith. "Would you like to do an interview with Harry, live, on tomorrow's show?" Pausing for a nanosecond to make sure I didn't have a better offer pending, I said, "Sure."

The next day I showed up at the appointed time, and reported to the second-floor roof from which all the TV outlets did their satellite feeds. I waited outside the broadcast tent on the roof for over half an hour. Finally the producer, looking somewhat sheepish, came around the corner and apologized that, "they just announced the Academy Award nominees, and I'm afraid we're gonna have to bump you."

"Never let it be said that a pending war got in the way of announcing the Academy Award nominees," I responded with as much irony as possible. He shrugged and apologized again. Yet another opportunity to present an alternative to Bush's rush to war was shot down.

Congressional Medal of Honor winner and Veterans For Peace member, Charlie Liteky (left), and Mike Ferner deliver a statement to a news conference at the Ministry of Information in late February 2003, announcing that the Iraq Peace Team will go to the Iraq-Kuwait border for a four-day fast, just three weeks before the U.S. invasion. (*Photo by Thorne Anderson*)

Incidents similar to this happened so often I quit noticing. One day I discussed the vast difference between our respective "back home" press coverages, with Neville Watson, a retired Australian minister who was part of our contingent. I told Neville about the second of two phone calls I made to my hometown newspaper, the *Toledo Blade*, and a Toledo radio station.

After accounting for the eight-hour time difference, managing to get through the hotel's rickety phone system, and then Baghdad's frail network, I reached the city desk at the Blade where I was told, "We're kinda busy right now. Can you call back later?" And a radio interview with morning show host, Denny Schaffer, sitting in the comfort of his downtown Toledo studio, ended with this acidic exchange.

"Don't you agree that sometimes ruthless thugs have to be dealt with? That we sometimes just have to go in and take care of things?"

"And just who should we 'take care of,' Denny? Should it be Ahmed, the kid who shined my shoes this morning, or Kamil, the hotel's tea-room manager who talked with me last night, or Mohammed, our cab driver today? Who do YOU think we should 'take care of,' Denny?"

Neville's experience had been quite the opposite. Two Australian TV stations and the *Sydney Morning Herald* covered nearly everything IPT did because of his participation with it, plus they did several feature stories on the Aussie who went to Baghdad. It seemed to me, I told Neville, that if the U.S. press did as good a job covering the peace movement as the Australian press, we wouldn't be going to war.

Neville was a veteran of Voices' efforts to end the sanctions and later to stop the war. He was in the group of a dozen of us who went to southern Iraq at the end of February, to fast for four days in the desert on the border of Kuwait.

In this final example of news media self-censorship, you be the judge. Was the U.S. news media's response to our trip to the Kuwait border an example of a consistent, massive failure to cover anything beyond Pentagon handouts, or were our actions simply not newsworthy?

Two days before we took one of the last Iraq Air flights out of Baghdad's Saddam International Airport to fly *through* the U.S. "no-fly" zone to the southern city of Basra and from there to drive to the Kuwait border, we held a news conference at the Ministry of Information in Baghdad to describe what we would do.

Reading our statement was Charlie Liteky, a member of the IPT delegation, and winner of the Congressional Medal of Honor in Vietnam, for rescuing twenty-two wounded GIs under fire, sustaining several wounds himself in the process. In 1985, he returned his medal, leaving it at the Vietnam Memorial in Washington, to protest U.S. policy in Central America, the only time in U.S. history that a Congressional Medal of Honor was returned by its recipient.

In the central room of the Ministry's press center, surrounded by over twenty IPT delegates from several nations, Charlie delivered the impassioned, eleventh-hour plea I had drafted for the team, consisting of two messages.

First, we pleaded with U.S. peace activists to begin massive sit-down protests. Secondly, we asked U.S. troops massed in northern Kuwait to think about the consequences of what they would be ordered to do; to consider whether they should obey. We told the reporters that our plan was to fly to Basra, drive an hour south through the last Iraqi village of Safwan to the border with Kuwait, and fast there for four days. During that time, we would give the statement Charlie had just read to the commander of the UN garrison at the border, and ask him to forward it to the U.S. command in northern Kuwait. We admitted it would likely not be distributed, but we wanted to do everything humanly possible.

When we arrived at the border, a large tent had been pitched for us less than 100 feet from a yellow line painted on the narrow, crumbling, two-lane asphalt road that crossed into Kuwait. (I should note that due to expected storms and since our tent had already been swept away by wind just prior to our arrival, our Iraqi hosts prevailed upon us to stay at a hotel in Basra, about a forty-minute drive north of the border.) Over that yellow line, U.S. troops would have to roll in an invasion. Beyond the line, the UN patrolled a narrow

Members of the Iraq Peace Team, during a four-day fast at the Iraq-Kuwait border, appeal to the U.S. peace movement to "Take a Risk, Sit Down for Peace," indicating the time is approaching midnight. From left: (kneeling, holding banner) Charlie Liteky; (sitting) Mike Ferner, Neville Watson, Ken Sehestead, Kathy Kelly, Cathy Breen, Sr. Virgine Lawinger, Cynthia Banas, Betsy Pasalaqua, (holding banner on far right) Cliff Kindy. (Standing) Ed Kinane, Doug Johnson, Chris Doucot, Peggy Gish, Rev. Jerry Zawada. (*Photo by Thorne Anderson*)

Neville Watson and Mike Ferner hold a banner in the two-lane roadway leading to the Kuwaiti border. In the background can be seen UN flags and trucks, part of the garrison staffing the "no-man's land" dividing Iraq and Kuwait. (*Photo by Thorne Anderson*)

"Voices" enlarged some of David Berrian's photos and took them to demonstrations throughout Baghdad the month prior to the U.S. invasion of March 20, 2003. Here they are displayed during the four-day fast at the Kuwaiti border. Several photos are taped to the Iraq Army's border checkpoint consisting of a tiny cement block shack (to the left, out of frame) and this arm, counterweighted with a rock, across the two-lane road that ran from the small Iraqi town of Safwan, to the Kuwaiti border. (*Photo by Thorne Anderson*)

"no-man's land" between Iraq and Kuwait. From our vantage point, we could see the flags of Iraq, the United Nations, and Kuwait.

The National Geographic Magazine was the only U.S. news media that came to report on our trip to the border, so from the only available public phone in Safwan, I called the network bureaus back in Baghdad. "If one of your crews in northern Kuwait comes to the Safwan border crossing, with a long lens they can get a shot of our tent from the Kuwait side," I urged them. "We have a huge banner that says 'TAKE A RISK! SIT DOWN FOR PEACE!' We'll be holding it this afternoon." Still nothing.

The next day, I called to tell them that Charlie and I would attempt to deliver our statement to the U.S. troops. At the appointed time, we walked up to the yellow line, careful not to put a toe over it, and hailed the UN guards. A Bangladesh Army captain and two sergeants walked slowly toward us until we could literally reach over the line, We shook their hands and give them the statement.

Knowing the statement was unlikely to find its way into the hands of U.S. GIs in Kuwait, we decided to make a more direct plea as well. We dragged a fifteen-foot piece of steel scrap up to the yellow line and helped 72-year-old Charlie Liteky climb it. With no amplification, but with a clear, deep voice on a cloudy, windless afternoon, Charlie read a letter referring to the statement we had just delivered, urging the troops to "visit our website and read all about it . . ." The shouts we heard back from the border guards assured us we had done as well as possible.

Chances are you did not see this drama on NBC News, or CNN, or in the *New York Times*, or hear it on NPR . . . or anywhere else for that matter. Those outlets were probably all busy interviewing the newly chosen Academy Award nominees.

Written with a drafting committee from the IPT in Baghdad, this is the statement that Charlie Liteky read at the news conference at the Ministry of Information, February 22, 2003, to announce our four-day fast at the Iraq-Kuwait border. It was also hand-delivered to the head of the UN garrison at the border, with the request that it be delivered to the commander of U.S. forces in Northern Kuwait.

To: U.S. troops in Northern Kuwait and to the U.S. peace movement

From: Iraq Peace Team, Baghdad
February 22, 2003

We, the Iraq Peace Team assembled here in Baghdad, recognize that we are indeed half past the eleventh hour for preserving peace and averting unimaginable suffering. Because the time remaining is so short and the stakes are so high, we are impelled to take uncommon measures. We ask people of goodwill, particularly our colleagues in the U.S. peace movement, to take uncommon measures as well.

On Monday, February 24, we will travel into the Demilitarized Zone along the Iraq—Kuwait border, across which 90,000 U.S. troops are ready to advance. There we will pitch a tent and conduct a four-day, water-only fast to focus the eyes of the world on our message directed to U.S. military personnel and to U.S. citizens.

First, to U.S. soldiers and sailors: our prayer for every one of you is for a quick return to families and loved ones without having to participate in the horrors of war. We recognize that you have been placed in a position full of anxiety and danger, and we share in the responsibility for you being here. We recognize you are in this position because back home we do not truly govern ourselves—but are instead ruled by a minority who decide questions of war and peace in the interests of the few instead of the many. Our inadequate democracy has led us into deadly quagmires in the past, and now to the brink of another conflict that can only be described as a tragic war of empire.

That tragedy, now within sight, will be all encompassing. The decisions we make in the next few days and weeks will forever change the lives of millions of people. Not only will you, our American brothers and sisters in the armed forces suffer greatly if war is waged, but so will the family we have come to know over many months here in Iraq—the common, decent, ordinary people who populate this country's cities and villages; who work in its shops and restaurants; go to school; practice their religion; celebrate birthdays and weddings and funerals; who, like the innocents in every war will bear the greatest suffering—-and who are virtually indistinguishable from our families back home, especially in their desire for peace. Indeed, it was General and President Dwight Eisenhower who told us, "Remember that all people of all nations want peace. Only their governments want war." We ask you, our fellow citizens, to think with your head and your heart and do the right thing.

And secondly, to those of you who marched in New York and San Francisco and Houston and Detroit and Peoria and a thousand other communities on February 15, we say this: our historic day of protest was not the end of our efforts, but only the beginning. With the hour terribly late and our leaders still ignoring us, the only thing that can avert war and a humanitarian disaster in Iraq is for people of conscience all over the United States to conduct a massive, preemptive sit-down for peace. It is time once again to use this non-violent, powerful, American-as-apple-pie recipe for justice that won unions for workers in the 1930's, civil rights for African-Americans in the 50's and 60's, and human rights for millions more.

This is our call, our appeal, our prayer from here in Baghdad to our friends and compatriots in the United States. Peace can still be preserved. Devastation can still be avoided. But you must go beyond what you think you can do. You must up the ante. With cataclysm hanging over our heads you must refuse to conduct business as usual. You must individually and collectively throw a giant wrench into the machinery of war. As Daniel Berrigan advised us, "the peace movement will only achieve success when it shows the same courage for peace as soldiers do for war."

We are capable of such courage. We must use it now.

◆ ◆ ◆

The international Peace Activists' joint statement, below was written with Ignacio Cano, a Spanish sociologist who came to Baghdad with the Human Shields on the overland route from England, on double-decker tour buses. We wrote it for a joint news conference held in the Andalus Hotel, on February 14, 2003, to announce a peace march that some 200 international activists would conduct the next day, in conjunction with larger marches held all over the world on February 15. The three groups issuing the joint statement were the IPT, the Human Shields, and Bridges to Baghdad, an Italian human rights group. Note: the "Iraq" spelling was the one more commonly used by international activists.

INTERNATIONAL PEACE ACTIVISTS' JOINT STATEMENT

Baghdad, Iraq
February 15, 2003

Different groups, composed of people from the U.S., Italy, Canada, Sweden, Ireland, Australia, Spain, Turkey, Poland, Norway, India, S. Korea, Great Britain, Slovenia and other countries are gathering here today to oppose this illegitimate war on Iraq and to spread the belief that peace is possible.

The fact that people around the world have left their homes and families and have made a long pilgrimage to Bagdad to express solidarity to the Iraqis in such difficult and dangerous circumstances is a clear indication of the deep and growing rejection that this war on Iraq is raising around the world. Each one of us who made it here represents thousands of our countrymen and women who share our feelings and want to work for a world where international law and peaceful negotiations prevail over the law of the strongest.

The people of Iraq have long suffered the consequences of armed conflicts and cruel embargoes. A war is the last thing the people of Iraq need now. A war is the last thing the world needs right now.

A war is the most serious decision a government can take and cannot be taken against the will of the people it is meant to be protecting. We ask you to help stop this war by stopping for one minute at noon every day, starting today, until the threat is over.

Statement issued February 15, 2003, in Baghdad, Iraq by:

Bridges to Baghdad   Human Shields   Iraq Peace Team

♦ ♦ ♦

3

JUST MINUTES UNTIL MIDNIGHT

After four days at the border and before heading back to Baghdad, we stopped in Basra to visit Bishop Kassab, head of the Chaldean diocese of southern Iraq. In perfect English, this gregarious Christian prelate told us what it was like tending a flock spread over such a huge area and thanked us for the suitcases of desperately needed medicines we brought with us. When I told the Bishop where I was from, he laughed and began naming some of my favorite Middle Eastern restaurants in Toledo and Detroit, places he had frequented during his trips to the United States over the years.

Turning to more serious matters, we asked him about the siren we had heard the previous evening followed by a distant explosion loud enough to rattle windows. He responded without hesitation that the blast was the fifth such detonation in the last two weeks, probably aimed at the same anti-aircraft battery just outside Basra that had been hit before.

A final highlight of our trip to the border was a scene that zipped past our car window as we drove through Safwan for the last time. Here's how I described it in a report home.

"In this southernmost village of Iraq, which endured such terrible damage and suffering 12 years ago (in the 1991 Gulf War as U.S. forces bombed Iraqi troops fleeing Kuwait), huge holes still gape in many buildings, vacant lots with rubble and standing water attract hapless gulls and egrets, and life is clearly, clearly a daily struggle. But in a little boulevard on the edge of town, a man was planting palm saplings in the earth. It was such a sign of hope that I couldn't ignore it. Hope that we can prevent a war, and hope on the part of this man and his village that they can replant their boulevard and enjoy it for years to come."

Back in Baghdad, my exit date of March 3 no longer looked so far away. I decided to take every opportunity to interview Iraqis.

One morning, Khalid, one of our regular cabbies, and I were on an errand. Pointing to the spider web of cracks in his windshield he asked, "Do you see how broken the window? Do you know that in 1991 I was living near the shelter, the Al-Amariyah shelter? When George Bush blow up shelter, my car close enough that all windows blow out except front window that cracks. I replaced all the other windows, and was going to replace front window. But now I think there will be another war so I wait."

Since just the two of us were in the taxi, I ventured a question I had not asked any other Iraqi. "What do you think of the Saddam Hussein government?" He scowled, turned his thumb down vigorously, and said "Shit. Shit! He takes money from everyone and puts in his pocket. From our pocket to his pocket. I am Shia. We don't like him." Then Khalid ended his comments the same way as did every Iraqi "We don't want a war."

It was now the end of February, nearing time for me to return home. Discussions at the IPT meetings were growing increasingly grim. Hans Blix reported midmonth that his inspectors had still not found any weapons of mass destruction and they wanted time to conduct further inspections, buoying us for a while. But within days, the Bush administration made it clear they didn't care what the United Nations said.

The IPT/Voices staff instructed us to make up "crash kits" with emergency water, food, and first aid supplies to keep by our doors in case an emergency evacuation to the basement bomb shelter was needed. Over the next couple of days, we formed committees to deal with contingencies including stockpiling bottled water and passing along basic first aid skills needed to treat casualties. The most sobering activity was filling out forms indicating our next of kin and, since Voices didn't have the funds to ship our bodies back to the United States, how did we want them disposed in Iraq?

People were told that if they were thinking of not staying through the war, they should probably leave while they still could. My return ticket was booked for March 3, just two days away. I knew that some of my new IPT friends would be staying no matter what, and that my new Iraqi friends, Kamil, the tea-room operator; Mohammed, our main "fixer" and driver; Fatima, the clerk at the stationery store; and Luray, the front desk manager at the Fanar simply had no other option. I felt a strong pull to stay, to do what I could to assist the wounded, and to make as much of a statement as I humanly could by my mere presence. On the other hand, I knew that I would be in an even better position to organize against the war if I returned home. It was a terribly difficult decision that I found myself on both sides of over a forty-eight-hour period.

In the end, I decided to go home and do what I could with my colleagues in the peace movement. On my last night in Baghdad, I attended a joint meeting of the IPT and the CPT delegations, about twenty-five people at that point. I knew in a few hours I would be getting on a plane at the Baghdad airport and the horrors they would soon experience firsthand I would only see as news reports on my TV back home. I listened to their quiet, firm voices discussing what the future might hold for them and the Iraqis. Searching for a way to honor their commitment, I expressed confidence that their efforts would one day be favorably compared with the early attempts to abolish slavery or win women's rights. I believed that 100 years on, people would look back at these brave souls who placed their bodies in harm's way, who had as much courage for peace as soldiers must have for war, and say, "So *that* was how humanity finally learned to abolish war!"

Razzaq Kazem al-Khafaj grieves over the bodies of his children on April 1, 2003 in Hilla, residential area of Nader, 80kms south of Baghdad, in the southern province of Babylon in Iraq. A total of 33 civilians were killed and 310 wounded when US-British coalition helicopters bombed the residential area; Khafaj lost a total of 15 family members (including six children) as they fled the region of al-Haidariyeh by car. (*Photo by Karim Sahib/AFB Photo/Getty Images*)

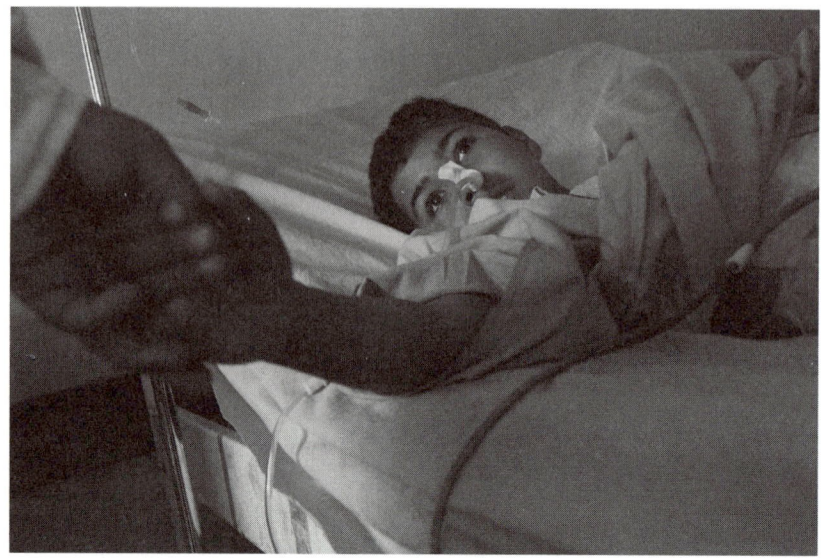

Omar Ali, 14, reaches for his father's comforting hand in the Al-Yarmouk hospital in Baghdad where he was treated for abdominal wounds from shrapnel. Doctors say twelve other members of his family were injured when a bomb landed near his home. Iraqi officials reported 207 civilian casualties from this, the second night of American airstrikes on Baghdad. (*Photo by Thorne Anderson/Corbis*)

I bought a notebook at Fatima's copy shop and reserved it for Iraqis to write short notes of whatever they wished to tell Americans. Some were written in English and some in Arabic. Here are the words of people from Basra, Safwan, and Baghdad to the outside world less than a month before the U.S. invasion of their country.

1. In the name of God the most Beneficent and Merciful.

   Warm Greetings. We are a loving peace people and we wish to live. We also hope that peace will exist in this region. We hate wars and believe that wars will never solve problems and that dialogue is the key for solving all problems.
   We pray to God that war never starts and request for peace to reign.

   > Resident
   > Qathem
   > Feb. 27. 2003

2. I am an Iraqi national.

   I pray to God to save us from the war because it's a disaster. We are a peaceful and freedom loving nation. In war there are no winner parties but a loss for all. I am saying this because I was a soldier in the war against Iran and I know the misery of war. If the USA government is greedy for oil then there are too many ways to have it by other means than war.

Feb. 26. 2003

3. In the name of God the most Beneficent and Merciful.

Letter to world nations.

We, the Iraqi peoples, love peace and would love to live in quiet and harmony like all nations in this globe without threat from any country.

We like to have an equal, loving, and peaceful relationship with all countries in the world.

We like all nations without exceptions, that is how our religion of Islam teaches us. It is a religion of forgiveness, love and peace.

As God said in the holy Quran, "in the name of God the Most Beneficent and Merciful" "No aggression except for the orbits" Professed God the Greatest.

Also God said: "In the name of God the Most Beneficent and Merciful" "wish for your brother as you wish for yourself" Professed God the Greatest.

We are nations with great civilization and honoured history though we argue that all honoured people in this world should stand in a positive position with the truth without being biased towards any party, no matter who they are.

Iraq/El Basra
Feb. 25 2003
Iraqi resident
Peace loving

4. I am an Iraqi national who works as a taxi driver with a group of people on long distance highways. I have a big family of nine people, three of them in the army and the other four are school students. Our economical situation is very difficult. We are uncomfortable at this time worrying and scared from the impending disaster of war that the USA will wage against us. We request of God to make the least damage out of this war and peace for the Muslims.
Peace upon you

Baghdad 9 a.m.
Feb. 23. 2003
Thank you so much

"In the name of God the Most Beneficent and Merciful"
"No power except for God the great" Professed God the Greatest.

5. "In the Name of God"

My name: Fatima

I like everyone and I have dreams like anyone but I can't do anything because the circumstances in my country. I'm finished my studies and in the holiday (4 weeks) I learned the computer and I want more to learn but I can't because we haven't money enough to learn and my husband want to learn the languages of English but he can't. We want travel to another cities but we can't do anything. I hope in the future we can do everything we want.

I wish good luck to everyone in the world.

At last I wish peace in all of the world and no more war.

My advice: Do not despair from the mercy of God. After the storm comes sunshine.

Feb. 18. 2003

6. You, Americans, are in peace there. I'm praying All Mighty God to continue this peace for you. But here in Iraq we are going through a painful and hard times, being in between: no war . . . no peace. Can you imagine that at every morning when I kiss my son Ali on his way to his college I begin praying to see him again . . . it is painful . . . still, we decided to defend our Iraq. We are defending no body and nothing except this Iraq which was the cradle of civilization. Let us shake hands and begin working for peace on the whole earth.

Best regards . . .
Nermin
Iraqi journalist
Feb. 23. 2003

7. In the name of God.

We are doing our best for peace and we believe on God to solve all the problem on the world.

To me I pray everytime for my country or for any one not to involve on the war because the war it's a bad things to all human beings. We love live and people and children and flowers with smile of the nature so we don't allowed to any body destroyed this beautiful nature not in Iraq but in any country in the world. Holy Quran said if any one make a fire to war God make it.

Thank you
Zaid
2003/2/27

8. We believe in peace because our profit said Al Slam Alykum meaning the peace is our life. We deal with it like food like the smile of child. When you cutting flower from the home it like that.

We don't like a war is bad disaster to any body. I hope American people believe on that and do their best of their brothers in Iraq to avoid the war not for my country but for all the region.

Peace. It is a wonderful world to live with.

Thank you

PART II

IRAQI VOICES AFTER THE INVASION

4

WELCOME
BACK TO BAGHDAD

Written on the first day of my return visit to Iraq: January 15, 2004.

Baghdad did not appear, to these Western eyes, as one of the prettier cities I'd seen when I first saw it before the war. Since then, weeks of intense bombing and ten months of occupation had taken a heavy toll. The sand and dust so prevalent in this desert city have, in modern times, been overcome by urban crud. This mixture coats everything: street signs, building facades, hotel windows inside and out, bathroom ledges, and the threadbare carpets of hotels where I live. It works its way into the coats of mongrels wandering the alleys until there's no such thing as a white cat or dog, just shades of dirty gray. It blankets cars, with the conspicuous exception of the venerable orange-and-white taxis whose owners bathe them at least daily.

Most noticeably, it coats the vegetation visible to a pedestrian. Whereas in some cities the greenery is actually green—even a bright, shiny green in the case of holly plants in warm climates—here it's not really green, but whatever color that's created by blending muddy gray and several verdant hues. When you realize that the palm trees and roadside shrubbery in this climate wear the same tired leaves year after year, you can almost hear the flora struggle to breathe.

Added to the urban desert grime is the omnipresent garbage piled and strewn in vacant lots, alleys, and street corners, most noticeably on the side streets connecting commercial arteries.

Then there are the rivulets and pools of liquid every twenty paces and at many street corners. As for what's in it, let's say it's better not to know entirely. I *can* report that in addition to the traditional mix of municipal water and sewage from ruptured pipes, occasional rain that's washed some of the grime out of the air and off buildings, and bits of refuse from street vendors—which includes in order of percent of content: vegetables, fruits, roasted chicken and lamb, raw chicken and lamb, falafel, nuts, soft drinks, tobacco, and shreds of office supplies and packaging—there are now considerable portions of gasoline, diesel fuel, and crankcase oil from innumerable generators used for standby electricity when the central power shuts down . . . the frequency and timing of which is another story altogether.

But it's what the occupiers have done to the lovely tree-lined boulevard of Abu Nuwas in a few short months of occupation that really tells a tale.

The fresh fish restaurants stretching for blocks on the Tigris River side of the street are all vacant, many vandalized. This noisy, gaudily lit portion of Baghdad nightlife is now quiet and deserted. The green spaces and occasional small parks, also on the river side of the street, are now mounded with bottles, cans, plastic bags, and stray trash, filled with ruts, and home for wandering dogs. I even saw a skinny, young mare and her colt wandering aimlessly down Abu Nuwas one day. Many of the trees have been knocked over or scarred badly.

On the other side of the street, there is no side of the street. For several blocks you can walk and see nothing but looming sections of twelve-feet high, concrete blast walls barely an arm's length away. At one point along this surreal walk, a concrete section was placed directly behind an inoperative traffic signal, making it look for all the world like the light might momentarily turn green and direct cars to drive straight into the wall.

This section of Pentagon beautification has been erected to protect the Sheraton and Palestine hotels from attack. Liberal applications of razor wire, floodlights, guard towers—complete with sandbags and young, private security guards brandishing Kalashnikovs—complete the image of an instant prison. Ironically, I was reminded of the "old regime days" as I started to take a picture juxtaposing the concrete wall and the sign atop the Sheraton. The guard yelled, "No picture, no picture!" I smiled as I pocketed my camera, thinking how some things haven't changed. At least in those days, when you got a stern warning for taking pictures, it was for focusing on something more sensitive than the back of the Sheraton Hotel.

Not many people walk this part of Abu Nuwas. Because the walls, towers, and razor wire do their job prohibiting traffic, because the fish restaurants are closed, and because only one residence remains inhabited, it is uncommonly quiet. It's one of the few places in central Baghdad where you can hear mourning doves, sparrows, and other birds singing. Cars are absent, as are their din and fumes and the need to be vigilant as you step from sidewalk to street. At the one occupied house, I heard a rooster crowing behind a privacy fence. Looking in for a moment, I saw two kids running in a tiny front yard.

On my first day back in town, I took this walk with a friend, Chris Doucot, a veteran of many trips to Iraq, to visit some of the staff we knew at the Al-Fanar hotel. Walking back, along Abu Nuwas, I watched as a bird of prey swooped to grab a mourning dove flying low. The two went to the ground and the dove was on its way to becoming lunch. The hawk saw us standing close by and took off, leaving the dove for later. Amid all the death and destruction, and given that this was nothing more than nature playing out its order, I wondered whether I should go to the dove's aid. At that moment, a young Iraqi man, who seemed to appear from nowhere, ran to the dove and picked it up. He spoke no English and I no Arabic, but we clearly had the same intention, to save the dove. He tried giving it a "start" into the air, but it flopped back to earth with a bad wing. So he brought it over and gave it to me, saying something I wish I understood, but it didn't sound like "bon apetit."

So there I stood, holding an injured mourning dove in the madness of Baghdad, walking back to a room that just that morning I'd been invited to share while I looked for permanent quarters—and no birdcage in sight. But I could feel the little bird's pulse beating under my fingers and I didn't know what else to do but help it live.

A couple of blocks after the concrete walls ended and the traffic pattern resumed, we walked past a vacant storefront complete with security gating. Inside, trash was piled high off to the side. Along one section of the gating, blankets and old curtains were hung to provide some privacy for a man and his four children who looked to be between two and ten years old.

Surprisingly, they were as lively and friendly as they were dirty and barefoot. They jumped up and down, waved, and said, "Hello, mister." Then they went wild when they spotted the dove nestled next to my chest. Of course they wanted to pet it; so I tried to make the experience as painless and

After a haircut and a complimentary beer, the author posed for a photo with the gang at a Karrada St. barber shop in Baghdad. (*Unknown photographer*)

nontraumatic for the frightened bird as possible. While I provided the kids an up-close view of nature, the father pulled back the gating and invited Chris inside for tea. They had a brief conversation and a small cup of the hot, sweet brew commonly extended in welcome and hospitality, and we continued on our way back to our lodgings.

We stopped by the apartment I was staying at so I could ask my generous host if by any wild chance there was a spare birdcage around. Her surprised, "No!" indicated she wasn't particularly interested in another guest, either.

We left to stroll the nearby commercial street, hoping to find something that would serve as a temporary sick room for my charge until it recovered. In the two blocks it took us to reach the commercial street, I felt the dove struggle a bit and gasp for air. A few moments later I could no longer feel its soft pulse. Down the block, a cat pawed through a pile of trash looking for food. I placed the dead dove near the cat and walked away.

"Welcome back to Baghdad," Chris said.

5

THE NEWS IN THE
NEW IRAQ

Directly across the Tigris River from the offices of the *Al-Mada* newspaper sit some of the hulks of presidential palaces and government buildings, heavily bombed from the U.S. shock and awe campaign and invasion. On the newspaper's side of the river, concrete blast walls and razor wire extend past its offices located on Abu Nuwas Street in central Baghdad.

Zuhair Al-Jezairy, assistant managing editor, ignored the scenery as he escorted his guest past a small parking area into a modest courtyard dotted with palm trees. Sitting on the back porch of a gracious, 100-year-old house renovated into newsrooms and offices, he explained the logistics of publishing a morning daily in Iraq.

"We depend on car travel to distribute the paper," he said, after confirming with his circulation manager that the workday begins at 3:30 A.M. for the four drivers. "We take first to the central Baghdad distribution center, and then to other main cities—from Basra in the south to Mosul in the north, all by 10:00." He acknowledged this schedule routinely results in speeding violations and "last month two accidents."

In production since July 2003, *Al-Mada*'s circulation is around 10,000, with occasional peak runs of 20,000 copies. "We are limited by our presses, and plan to install more of them soon," the wiry, 58-year-old newsman stated. The mention of press capacity leads to the first discussion of the ousted Saddam Hussein government.

"Many presses belonged to the old government and religious parties, and several newspapers got access to them right after the war," he said, adding that "the intelligence services had the modern printing presses. All the other ones were older, from the 1970s."

Not long after the former government was toppled by the U.S. invasion, he said that newspapers sprang up by the score. "Under Saddam Hussein there were only three main papers, one for the Ba'ath Party, one for the Kurdish party, and one for the government, but they had essentially the same news and layout. Right after Saddam's government fell, we had over 100 papers, but some of them lasted only for a few issues."

This explosion of newspapers magnified the shortage of printing presses and a shortage of journalists. Al-Jezairy recalled that "there had been two waves of emigration of intellectuals, in the late 1970s and again during the Iran–Iraq war and the sanctions."

He recalled that in 1976, the government decreed that media and culture should fit in with Ba'ath Party ideology. Writers and others were required to sign a form stating they were joining the Ba'athists or at least refusing to join any other political organization, "forcing many journalists to leave." Those who stayed were eventually circumscribed by the Saddam Hussein dictum, "It is not necessary for writers to report everything they know." Al-Jezairy left Iraq in 1979, remembering that Hussein was nominated for president on July 18 of that year. "I left a few days before," he smiled grimly.

Covering the Lebanese civil war and other hot spots kept him busy for several years, earning him the nickname "correspondent of the boiling point," as he worked under contract for such newspapers as Al-Hayat, Al-Hurria, and Al-Safeer.

The next stop for the soft-spoken journalist was as senior producer for Associated Press Television News, a job that took him to the United States three times in the mid '90s. "Once was to do a feature on Islam and the West, one to cover the U.N. financial crisis, and one," he said, barely repressing a laugh, "was to cover the O.J. trial in Los Angeles."

Keeping his hand in electronic media meant he also produced television documentaries on subjects like Saddam Hussein's family, a four-part series now airing on Al-Arabia TV, a documentary on Africa, and one on his own return to Iraq from London last year.

Returning to the vagaries of journalism in today's Iraq, Al-Jezairy explained that "the older generation of reporters came from literature. Most of the newer generation had a two-year training in Baghdad University's media college where they learned to write only short reports—and under Saddam Hussein they had to depend on his phrases to praise war and soldiers. That's my problem with reporters today, they can't criticize. But that is beginning to change now and the cover is coming off."

Answering the frequent question, "was the war worth it?" Al-Jezairy responded, "To me it's a complicated feeling. As a writer and human I can't accept the war as a way to solve a problem but it was unfortunately the only way to get rid of Saddam. Most of the people I met think yes it deserves the high price of war and the situation after. There are some worries that the occupations will take longer time than they expected, and the American solders with their tanks in the streets increasing their daily problems."

Two other difficulties facing his reporters were a lack of official sources and an abundance of rumors, both worsened when the government fell last April and documents were looted and burned. "Even official sources often do not have documents. This makes it difficult in many things, for example, when many people claim to own the same home. Even new owners print their own documents sometimes." His paper tries to overcome this problem by requiring that reporters get confirmation from three sources.

Al-Mada's biggest story, and one of the biggest to rock post-war Iraq, was dubbed the "Oil for Loyalty" series, a take-off on the UN's oil-for-food program allowed under the sanctions.

Oil for Loyalty chronicled corruption of international proportions. "It has affected people from Nazis to Communists, to churches, to members of parliament, to elites in France, Bulgaria, Hungary, Jordan, Switzerland, and the son of the symbol of Pan Arabism, Gamal Abdel-Nasser," enumerated the feisty editor. "Some people were our friends, but we have to tell the truth."

The paper kicked off the story in February 2004 by publishing a list of 175 people who benefited from Saddam Hussein's illegal largesse. A small and often undocumented network of top administration officials rewarded political parties and individuals around the world for loyalty to the Hussein government with "coupons" for millions of barrels of Iraqi oil smuggled out of the country under the noses of UN inspectors and sold on the open market, using a special account in Iraq's Al-Rafidain Bank. He said his paper could likely prove even wider complicity in the corruption but for the lack of official documents.

"The story had been unofficially known for some time by many people, but never proven until the government fell last year," Al-Jezairy said. "Since we broke the story we have been threatened with lawsuits from many, many people around the world; the Iraqi Governing Council has begun meeting weekly on the subject to try and get some of the money back; and the international press has been very interested. Sometimes we give over twenty interviews a day and might have five or six journalists waiting in the office." He added that this was only his second interview by an American journalist, however.

Asked what he saw in the future for his paper, Al-Jezairy quickly answered, "new printing presses," followed by a description of the kind of issues *Al-Mada* will be known for. "We will cover the effort to get rights for women and other important political stories. There is a lot of interest in Saddam Hussein's family, and in crime. Several other papers concentrate on this, but not *Al-Mada*."

The new addition to the Abu Hanife mosque consists of this cemetery for people killed in a battle with U.S. troops two days after the Saddam Hussein government was ousted, including this one for a neighborhood youth, Ali Amer Ibrahim Al-Jobori, reportedly shot by U.S. troops, April 11, 2003. (*Photo by Mike Ferner*)

A view of the interior of Abu Hanife, the largest Sunni mosque in Baghdad. (*Photo by Mike Ferner*)

6

BAGHDAD
COLLEGE HIGH SCHOOL

Their textbooks were photocopied and ragged, but they were still in English, and the students were still proud that their school was founded by the "American Fathers."

With a name like Baghdad College High School (BCHS), you might expect it's a college-prep institution, but nearly everything else about it is completely unexpected—from its Jesuit roots to the very fact that it survives today. Recently added to its many distinctions is the fact that it is very likely the only school in Iraq with high-school "pen friends" in the United States.

Those pen friends, as the Iraqi students call them, were from two secondary schools in Toledo, Ohio: Jesup W. Scott, a venerable, inner-city institution belonging to Toledo Public Schools, and St. John's Jesuit, founded by the same order of Roman Catholic priests as BCHS.

I asked two teachers at these schools if their students might like to exchange letters with students their own age living in Baghdad. They jumped at the chance and supplied me with a couple of dozen letters from each school.

Back in Baghdad, Dahr Jamail introduced me to a friend of his, Ghazwan Al-Mukhtar, a gruff, chain-smoking Iraqi who had attended UC Berkeley and graduated from the University of Wisconsin. His youngest son was a student at BCHS and Ghazwan was happy to introduce me to his boy and to "the best high school in Iraq."

In 1932, he told me, Jesuit priests from the United States founded the English language school and built a church on adjoining property. When the Jesuits left in 1969, the church was turned over to priests from an ancient Middle-eastern Christian sect, the Chaldeans. In the mid '70s, the school was nationalized and became part of Iraq's state school system. According to several BCHS instructors, it was considered the top school in the Hussein government's Gifted School Program initiated in 1999.

The school grounds are still beautiful, but a dozen years of economic sanctions and three wars have left the buildings with the same look of dusty exhaustion prevalent in so much of this ancient city. Along with the school's physical plant, its academic standards have also eroded. Edicts from Saddam Hussein coupled with Iraq's growing economic crisis following the U.S. invasion are taking a toll. Teachers and the school's dean admitted that few students come to BCHS able to speak English these days, fewer teachers are able to teach in English, and orders from Saddam prohibiting anyone from speaking to a school principal in a foreign language have contributed to the changes.

On a campus tour, our first stop was a small storage building filled with textbooks. Picking one up at random, I noticed it was an 1,100-page calculus book, published in 1990, or rather, a ragged photocopy of a 1990 calculus textbook. Abdullah Hashim, the librarian in charge of issuing textbooks, explained that 1,000 photocopies of the book were made in Jordan and brought back to BCHS in 1994. Each year, about 100 copies simply wore out, so they expected to be out of usable calculus texts soon.

Already, Mr. Hashim sighed, 150 students lacked Algebra textbooks, and Biology students were lucky to have a photocopied 1984 edition, since many copies burned when the Ministry of Education was looted immediately after the U.S. military took control of Baghdad in April 2003. With pride he showed me one bright spot in his inventory: some surplus copies of a French language textbook imported the previous year for tenth and twelfth graders.

For a month after the United States captured Baghdad, Ghazwan explained, troops occupied the school. Military vehicles were parked on soccer fields and tennis courts and classes were cancelled, although most teachers continued to show up every day.

Walking towards the art department, Ghazwan lamented the "incomprehensible vandalism" the school suffered at the hands of U.S. troops.

"They looted 120 computers," he said angrily. "They took the CPUs and just broke the monitors. They knocked over all the shelves in the library, throwing books everywhere. Even after ending their occupation of the school, the troops returned for 'inspections.' They emptied desks and cabinets, tossing everything on the floor. We put it all back and the troops returned the next day and did the same thing."

In one of the art classrooms remained proof of the damage Ghazwan said was done by the conquering troops: a blackboard spray-painted with what appeared to be American gang symbols and the words "Soth Side." On another wall, a student's large watercolor painting had been sprayed with the words "Fuck Saddam."

Fa'az Majid, BCHS art supervisor, described a raid conducted by U.S. troops in his classroom one morning when the contents of his cabinets were "all thrown on the floor, but nothing was taken." Vandalism by U.S. troops was not the only destructive force to hit the school recently, he added.

"The 'de-Ba'athification' carried out by the Coalition Provisional Authority cost us already four of our best, most experienced teachers," Majid said. "Students demonstrated. They cried because they had lost very valuable teachers."

Added Ghazwan, "the so-called 'de-Ba'athification' of teachers is irrelevant. When that teacher stands in front of a geometry class, he doesn't give the Ba'ath Party view of a triangle, he teaches geometry. Our students are losing valuable teachers as a result of this stupid policy."

While we waited for Dean Jacob Joseph to finish a meeting, Ghazwan hailed Abdel Hussain Umaran, a remarkably fit, 70-year-old physical education instructor who still played basketball. As part of his introduction, Mr. Umaran said with obvious pride that "in 1963 when I was a young man," he had won admittance to a university in Texas but had been unable to attend. Then he recounted an incident he said happened two months earlier.

"U.S. Army soldiers came in with a number of 'Iraq Today' newspapers (Baghdad's English language daily), asking for permission to distribute them. I told him I would have to ask the administration first. But the soldiers right away said, 'you're creating a problem,' and handcuffed me in front of my students. One of my students complained, and they handcuffed him as well. Later they took me outside and apologized."

The former Iraqi 800-meter champion added that, "the Marines who were first here were much better than the soldiers now. They treated us with dignity, allowed us into school freely, shared their food, and were much more friendly. I know the soldiers have been attacked, but that is no reason to mistrust us."

Dean Joseph arrived, inviting us to the library, where we were soon joined by Mudhaffar Hasu, a BCHS English teacher, Mr. Al-Nasseb, the schools's head math instructor, and Mr. Samira, head of Social Studies.

Mr. Al-Nasseb corroborated what I heard earlier regarding vandalism committed by U.S. troops. "They broke many things. They wrote on the walls, dirty things. In the end we don't like them. We changed a dictator but for imperialism. We have heard about your democracy but we haven't seen it."

Mr. Samira added that "all my maps were torn down, glass broken." To which Dean Joseph lamented, "And my poor biology lab. My poor biology lab."

The dean added that he would rather close the library because it had a water leak in the heating system and there was no money for repairs. In the meantime, "I am using my own money" to keep it going.

Turning the topic to the broader effects of the war and its aftermath, Dean Joseph said, "Things are improving now, but not the terrorists. And Americans cannot distinguish between an Iraqi and a terrorist, so they commit terrible mistakes. For example, my daughter works at a company that makes equipment for agriculture and irrigation. Two tanks attacked the company. Why? This makes people more anxious. I agree Iraqis want liberation, but what came after April was very bad."

"Look," the administrator added, "I had a brother, a cousin and a nephew executed by the old regime. When they killed my brother I had to pay 25 Iraqi dinar (about $70 at that time) for his coffin and the bullets they used . . . and

I am one of millions. Saddam Hussein is a beast and a monster, so yes, I wanted to get rid of him. But am I now getting better? Yes and No. I have the right to speak, but . . .

"This is all," finished the math department head, Al-Nasseb.

Dean Joseph nodded in agreement and went on to comment about economic conditions, saying they were "not sufficient for living, only for survival. Compared to people in other Mideast countries we are very poor."

(His description today would undoubtedly be much bleaker. Electric service, expected to resume to prewar levels has instead gotten worse. Central Baghdad residents consider themselves lucky to get power five hours a day, frequently in the middle of the night. Drivers sleep in their cars overnight to keep their place in five-mile-long lines at petrol stations snaking all over Baghdad. Fuel prices have increased several times over and inflation is driving up the cost of basic foods.)

As sunlight slanted through the library window and a haze of smoke, Dean Joseph drew a thoughtful drag on his cigarette and observed, "The cost of getting rid of Saddam Hussein was cheap, but the Iraqi people are now suffering and expect more suffering. I expected to live in some prosperity in my last days but I don't think so now. The Americans created Saddam Hussein and the Americans got rid of Saddam Hussein. But the Iraqi people in the new regime have no jobs and that's why there are terrorists."

Al-Nasseb, the math instructor, concluded with a criticism of his own, mixed with a note of pride about his beloved school. Western news reports after the fall of Baghdad "concentrated on the looting and burning. They didn't show us teaching students in the open air because the baccalaureate exams were coming."

7

FROM "KEEP YO HEAD" TO "GOD BLESS US ALL": U.S. AND IRAQI STUDENTS BEGIN A CONVERSATION

Tucked in a suitcase for my second trip to Iraq was a stack of letters written by students at two Toledo high schools: Jesup W. Scott, one of the oldest in the Toledo Public Schools system, and St. John's Jesuit, a Catholic, all-boys school. I delivered them to teachers at BCHS. They invited their students to respond to the Toledo students and, when I returned, I took those letters with me to deliver to the teachers in Toledo.

What follows are four pairs of complete letters between the Toledo and the Baghdad students, and random excerpts from several other letters. Some students' names have been changed.

◆ ◆ ◆

January 12, 2004

To Whom It May Concern:

My name is Peter and I am currently completing my third year of High School in Toledo, Ohio where I was born and have lived my entire life. I enjoy reading, playing sports and hanging out with my friends. I have a part time job which takes up much of my time and I also have many chores that I have to do around the house. I am very curious to learn about the events that are currently taking place in your country. Your country is constantly a topic of discussion in the U.S. and information about your country is often on the news. However the information

I receive may be biased and I am very eager to learn the true story. With all the different information that I receive it is difficult for me to decide whether or not if I support the United State's decision to enter Iraq. At times it seems like we are doing a good thing, but at others it seems like we are disturbing your nation and we are in a place we do not belong. I am curious to know your position on the United State's decision to enter Iraq. . . I hope you have learned something about the United States from my letter and I also hope that your nation is successfully rebuilt.

Sincerely,
Peter

♦ ♦ ♦

March 8, 2004

Dear Peter,

Thank you for your letter which I think I'm lucky to receive. I'm Rami, a 17-year-old student in Baghdad College high school. I like sports especially soccer and I like computers very much. I like hanging out with friends but these days we can't because of the security problems. I'm always good in school and my friends say that I study too much. OK enough talking about me and let's get into business.

I'm gonna talk about the every day life here and you can understand the situation in Iraq which as you said is in the spotlight right now and an open land for making up false news. It's like journalists get money for the number of words they make each day. Life here starts at 7:00 A.M and ends about 10:00 P.M. Nobody dares to go out after that time and only robbers or American soldiers are seen in the streets. But before that time you see people in streets trying to live their life as humans (but sometimes they can't) and ignore the sounds of explosions and bullets which became usual every now and then. But the best subject now is the new constitution and how the governing council members never get to solve their problems. Me . . . I'm now a special expert in determining the sounds of weapons and telling their distance (range) and like everyone else a politician talking and analyzing like some kind of professor. About my opinion of the American entrance to Iraq. I don't really support that decision. And although it ended a brutal dictatorial regime it brought the American occupation which the Iraqis can't stand. Some soldiers don't know much about our traditions so they made a lot of mistakes which caused the armed resistance that killed and injured many soldiers (much more than the announced one). Security is not a matter of discussion. Why? Cuz there is no security and the reason for that is the heavy flow of foreigners through the open borders which can't be controlled. As a whole the situation is neither as bad as what Al Jazeera (the Arabic news channel) says nor as good as what Fox news says. So take my advice . . . switch the TV to the Comedy Channel and forget about it. I don't have a stance for George Bush but I think the US deserves a better president.

OK I've been talking too much but I hope that you got a clear view about what's going on here and I hope we become friends.

Yours,
Rami

♦ ♦ ♦

Dear Iraqi Student,

Hi, my name is Justen. I'm a senior at Scott High School. I want to tell you how I feel about how our country is bombing yours. I think its so very wrong that Bush started this war with no real idea on what he was looking for. Many of our soldiers, and many of your innocent bystanders died for no reason. You guys over there probably don't like Bush and we don't either. I think he started this war just to get the support of more of the American people, but in actuality I think he has more people hating him.

I think he has his priorities all messed up. I guess he thinks he accomplished something by capturing Saddam. I don't believe he anything but waste millions on a useless war. That money should've been going toward our schools system, we need it dearly.

I guess I'm trying to say I agree with you all I think. Have a nice life.

Sincerely,
Justen

♦ ♦ ♦

Dear Justen,

Hi, my name is Abdullah. I'm a senior at Baghdad High School. First I'd like to thank you for you sensitive letter, it really made me feel happy.

Well, I live in Baghdad Since 1987 and I spent my god and bad times in it. It was a great city but a lot of wars destroyed it and ruined it. may be you don't know why all this happened, but let me tell you that it was because of the oil, that damned liquid made a lot of people die for nothing and a lot of nations fight for it. Well, the last war was for this purpose, it wasn't for capturing Sadam only. you know Bush wasted his millions to earn oil from Iraq, that was his idea. Many of your and our soldiers died and a lot of kids and innocent people burried under their houses.

So all we want is peace on this beautiful earth. Peace is our dream. now I'm writing to you at 12.45 A.M and I can't write any more. Justyn I wrote to you with an openedheart. So I want you to send me messages on this email box: crazy-guy@_____.

Yours Sincerely,
Abdullah

♦ ♦ ♦

Dear Iraq Student,
Hello, how are you doing? My name is Shaneel and I live in Toledo, Ohio. I attend Jesup W. Scott high school, in Toledo. I am in the 12th grade, I play sports for my school. My favorite sport is basketball, and I plan on attending college next fall on a scholarship for basketball.

Even though I am a United States citizen, I feel that it's majority our fault about everything that is going on. The United States government is entirely too noisy, and their always in somebody else business. "but I still love my country," but I feel that our lives our in danger, and that all of us need to just settle this, well our governments need to settle their differences between themselves. So we can continue our peaceful lives as citizens.

Shaneel
8/3/2004

♦ ♦ ♦

Dear Shaneel,
My name is Ali. I'm glad to write to you. I'd received you letter it was the first letter I recive from person.

I'm 17 years old, I was born in Samarra 120 km north of Baghdad. I've 2 sisters. I'm in the 5th class I spend most of my spare time watching TV and using my computer. I like LA Lakers and Boston Celtics My favourite sport is football. I was so sad when my team refuse me to join the club so I decided to play basketball But I think it's a difficult game.

I usually stay at home reading and watching football matches with my father. I saw yesterday a football match between Inter and Roma in the Italian League. I was sad because my team (Inter) had lost 1–4. I used to play football with my neighbours, but one of them had been kidnapped.

Life is miserable here. no electricity. no clubs, and no security. I've beautiful friends in my class, one of them makes jokes on teachers and the other had lost his eye and part of his face by a bomb.

Summer is very hot in Iraq specially without electricity. I can speak French. One time I spoke to a French person.

Thank you very much for your letter and I hope that situation in Iraq changes. Have a good time with your family and friends.

Ali
January 12, 2004

♦ ♦ ♦

Dear Friend,

My name is Chris. I attend high school in Toledo, Ohio and I am the oldest child in my family. I have one brother and one sister, both younger than I am.

In writing this letter I hope to find answers to some questions that I have pertaining to Iraq and the war. Here in the United States, President Bush recently asked Congress to grant him $87 billion dollars to help rebuild Iraq, a process that is expected to take several years, and they granted his request. As an individual, do you agree with the united States' involvement in the rebuilding of your country or do you wish that American troops withdraw and allow the citizens of Iraq to rebuild it in their own way? Due to American involvement in the destroying of Saddam Hussein and his regime, do you think that anti-American sentiment is stronger than it was before or do you feel that the United States has gained support from the citizens of Iraq? Many anti-war Americans felt that Bush hastily invaded Iraq without enough evidence to support that Saddam possessed weapons of mass destruction. Do many people in Iraq feel that America invaded and overthrew Suddam Hussein and his regime because of the very realistic threat that he posed, or do you feel, like some Amercans that it was simply for oil and economic purposes? Do you and others believe that Saddam did in fact possess weapons of mass destruction or do you feel that he was telling the truth when he repeatedly denied to the world that he possessed any such weapons? . . . I thank you for taking the time to read my letter and greatly hope that you answer my questions as best you can.

Sincerely,
Chris

♦ ♦ ♦

Dear Chris,

My name is Bashar, I'm 16 years old, I attend high school in Baghdad called Baghdad College, and I'm the middle child in my family. I have one brother older than me and one sister younger than me. I'm so glad to receive a letter from you. But I receive your letter too late so I don't have much time to answer all the questions and I hope that I can answer some of them and the rest of your questions I will answer them through the email when I receive your email address from you and my email is _____.

The rebuilding of Iraq is an Iraqi matter and there are no problems to participate in it all the countries, not only the countries that involve in the war on Iraq, and the involvement of USA should be discuss with Iraqi people because America invade Iraq.

It's not the matter of Saddam having or not having mass destruction weapons, Saddam would not be dangerous to USA if he had got these weapons because USA could destroy Iraq in minutes. USA was never threated by Iraq, except in the pretending of American administration.

I believe that America is very interested to have the control of oil and to whom it would be bought, that's mean a basic factor in the international politic of United States.

This is a short answers and we can talk more in email as I told you above.

Sincerely,
Bashar
8th March 2004

◆ ◆ ◆

Dear Robert,

I was very pleased and delighted when I read your letter, it's comforting to know that there is someone out there thinking about you. I thank you very much for your sympathies and I would like you to know that you did lift my spirit up.

I am having a bad time in my daily life, actually going anywhere without being in danger is nearlly impossible. There are explosions, gunshots and cross fire everywhere, it's like old Texas and a lot worse. I just wanted you to know nothing but a few of our problems and off course no need to mention cutting of electricity and the passing of large noisy tanks all the time (24–7) . . . aking the house tremble as they pass.

. . . if you have a computer you can email me if you want to at BlueKnight@_____, but you must know that I must go to an Internet café to open my box. (Phone lines and building were bombed during the war.) I like studying languages too, one by one. right now I'm studying French and English off course and wish to continue.

About the war, Sadamm and your President Mr. George Bush, it is all a game my friend, it has been planned for long time ago. that's what we think . . . and don't be sorry. it's not your fault that we were invaded, we are living in a world where "Power and Money" is the vital element that is running the show. Military troops were sent to Iraq for oil and other purposes that a few people know.

In spite of all the problems and dangers we live in I decided to carry on my own good life (I hope) and for a better promising future since Sadamm's rule was over. I am and will stay focused forever and ever. won't taste rest untill all my dreams shall come true with God help. woo! sorry I got excited a bit.

. . . I do have many relatives aboard especially in the United States, and I made some friendships with U.S. soldiers (they are nice people and they feel home sick) . . . Any way, this case is special I always wanted to communicate with people of my age in U.S. If you feel bored why don't you have some fresh air and drink something warm (I don't know what kind of weather exactly in Ohio now!) and sorry for the mistakes I made it's dark and there is no electricity so I have to use the chargable light.

I really hope that you send me back but if you don't like to I will understand don't worry. Thank you again and I think that you are a good person. God bless us all.

> Sincerely,
> Mohammed
> The Blue Knight

◆ ◆ ◆

Dear Christopher,

. . . OK now let's talk about you I need more detail about you and your family. If you can send me your family picture. Send me your email if you have. We the students must be opened to the world. as you read as you know that the Iraqi person relates with different kind of people. please don't judge in what you watch in the TV. take this advice "the tolerance about what happened to you makes you choose the right way."

> Sincerely,
> Hassan
> P.S "laugh to life the life will laugh to you"
> 9th March 2004 Baghdad

◆ ◆ ◆

Dear Krystle,

My name is Amer. I am a senior at Baghdad College. I'd like to thank you about your feelings against the occupation of Iraq and against your president Mr. Bush, who made many faults when he decided to invade Iraq, and the Iraqi people and American soldiers pay for his faults . . .

I think the problem is that in your democracy, you can talk everything and the government do whatever they want.

◆ ◆ ◆

Dear Eric,

. . . My school is well known as the best and the most stressful school in the whole country . . . My favorite sport to watch and play is football (soccer) . . . My favorite movie actor is Mel Gibson and my favorite actress is Michelle Pfeiffer.

I also listen to music, mostly Arab music but sometimes I listen to American music. My favorite Arab singer is Kadim Al Saher who was rewarded in BBC Music Awards . . . My favorite American group of singers Backstreet Boys and especially Howie Dorough.

Saddam Hussein was not a very good man but, however, he is better than those who are governing the country right now. The US army should not be in Iraq now because the war was with a meaningless reason. They said that President Saddam had weapons of mass destruction, but they had not found these weapons. So the speeches of George Bush and Tony Blair were all lies.

About the US soldiers, there are a few who are good and friendly, but most of them are bad and barbaric and you can really call the terrorists in the true meaning of the word, when you see their treatment to Iraqi people when they enter houses to search for weapons (even when they know that there are no weapons in that house) and when you see that they do not respect Iraqi people at all, even some of them stole money and gold pieces when they found them in the houses I have mentioned. So, you can't blame Iraqi people when they attack your soldiers (and Iraqis are well known by their courage), and if you've seen what the soldiers have done in Al Anbar governorate I can say that you might have come and join the resistance yourself (but don't think that I've joined the resistance).

. . . We were also split about capturing Saddam Hussein: some people were glad and celebrated in streets and others were very sad and even cried when he appeared on TV in this miserable picture.

. . . Finally, I would like you to know that when I used the term (The Americans) I don't mean the American people because we all know that there's a big difference between people and administration.

Sincerely,
Ahmed

♦ ♦ ♦

Dear Austin,
My name is Husam, I'm 17 years old . . . my father is a teacher of math at Baghdad university, and my mother is a doctor. I spend most of my time on computer and Internet; I also play football and billiards. now I finished to you my profile.

About your question, I won't answer them all, because I don't like the political affairs, I don't want to say anything on this subject, and I will tell you about our climate only. The climate in Iraq in one word is dry, hot in summer, very cold in winter . . .

Now I want to ask you that why you don't speak enough about your study level, your hobbies, how do you spend your time . . . Do you love music? Do you know any Arabic singer? How about your relation with the females (this is an important question, I want you to answer in precise details if you answer my letter).

At the end, I wish that you felt happy when you read my letter. And I wish that you became my penfriend.

Sincerely,
Husam

♦ ♦ ♦

Dear Iraqi student
My name is Christopher and I always woundered how it be to have a Iraqi friend. I also woundered how it is to live over seas. Like what is it like to live with major problems going on in your country. I can't say I know what your going through. If I could relate to what you would be going threw. No matter what happens don't give up at what every you are try to do in your life. You life is very vauleable to you and if you give up you might as well be dead or nothing cause if you can make in whats going on now I think you can make it through any thing.

Sincerely,
Chris
P.S. Keep yo head

♦ ♦ ♦

Dear Brandon,

My name is Wael . . . I like swimming and I hear music, specially Beyonce, Jennifer, Christina, Britney, Madonna and Westlife and of course Michael Jackson. I hope to go to an excited Beyonce party but of course I can't. My best song is "Crazy in Love" by Beyonce. Surely I'm glad that Saddam is out of power now . . . we can use the internet, the mobile and the satellite. . .

I don't like Bush and I don't like Saddam. I think that the war was a very big mistake and I think that there aren't any nuclear weapons. But tell me, what do you think about Beyonce? And what is your favourite singers and songs? I really hate the rap! What about you? I'm so glad that I received your letter, Brandon, and I really enjoy writing to you. I hope to hear from you soon. Thank you and Good bye.

Sincerely,
Wael

♦ ♦ ♦

Dear DJ,

You said that the most you get to to see about the war is what news on the TV. I think the most favorite channel you watch the news of the war on is (CNN). I advise you to watch some neutral channels, this will give you a better picture about the war because what you see on the (CNN) and other American channels is not very real . . .

The American troops are making the situation in Iraq worse than before because of their gorilla style. They use to make it better in Iraq. I want to tell you that one of our legal right is the resistance, by the way, I'm not talking about the terrorist activities against the Iraqi. But about resistance against foreign invasion on our land that is one of the human rights . . .

Let's take for example your ally the British when the Germans attacked it they defended against it and your country, you hit the civilians in Japan with nuclear bombs because they attacked a military harbour . . . In the end I would like to say that Iraq is a beautiful country and his people are a friendly people but powerful, too, and don't let any one give you another picture about us. My address is _____.

I hope you contact me soon after you will receive my letter on the address that has been mentioned before. And I hope we will become pen friends.

God bless you,
Mustafa
3/8/04

♦ ♦ ♦

Dear Jevonne,
I am a male my name is Mohamed age 17 from Baghdad, Iraq . . . I have two Brothers and a mum and dad.

When the U.S. Army Bombed Iraq It was 5 A.M when I woke up on the sound of the explosive of rockets and Bombs. At that day a series of awful horrible days began, each night the B-52 Bomber bombed Baghdad at about 11:30 P.M thousands of bombs were dropped on Baghdad and a very hard explosive and many innocent people were die. Many buildings near my house were bombed and that was very scary, a lot of splinters dropped near the house. The hospitals was very bad and no medicine was there.

The war is a bad thing. It all destruction and ruination we love the peace. The Islam and Arabic people call for the peace. We know that the American people and most of the U.S. Army have no thing with what happened in Iraq and hate the war.

◆ ◆ ◆

Dear Iraqi,
My name is Steven. I'm 17 years old and I attend my last year of high school. Just so that you know not every American feels the whole war was just. I can't picture myself hearing bombs and gunshots out side my house with out being scared . . . The 500-plus soldiers that have died is a tragedy but I know the number of people killed there doesn't compare. Being a black male in the country of freedom I know that I myself don't receive fair treatment so god knows what is going on there . . . if the misunderstandings between our cultures could be over soon none of the would happen and instead of sending a letter we could see each other without fear or worry of a problem.

◆ ◆ ◆

Dear American student,
Hi, my name is Ibrahim . . . I have three sisters, Dad, Mum and a small dog. I've received your letter that makes me feel that many people remember us. . . I believe as you believe and the world too that we don't have any biological or chemical weapons since the Second Gulf War, but what can I say? I hope to see more beautiful days than I've seen since the day I was born because I believe in the words said by a French writer but I don't remember his name at the moment, nevermind, he said that "All wars are civil wars because all men are brothers."

. . . Where do you live? Do you have a brother or a sister? Do you have a pet? What do you do at your spare time? What's your favourite sport? and do you like video games? I wish you could write to me because I have many things to tell you about myself, friends, adventures and HUG.

Sincerely,
Ibrahim

♦ ♦ ♦

Dear Jay,
. . . you think your country is here for controlling our oil and therefore providing energy for you i think that you're right but no one prevent your country from buying our oil and i don't think its about oil only cause the united state has most of the saudian and kuwaitian and qutarian oil. I think it's more than that.

But finally I would like to say that you and I are both the future and it's leaders so beeing friends better than beeing enemies and finally I happy cause i received your letter and I wish you good luck and to all your friends and if there was a next time in writing letters to each other please don't write in cursive it was so difficult form me to understand your word.

thank you and au revoir
Yours faithfully
Ahmed
March 7, 2004

♦ ♦ ♦

Dear Anthony,
How do you do? I was very delighted when I received your outstanding letter . . . And now I'll follow your style in writing. It seems from your letter that you're interested in politics (especially war on my country), well, I gotta tell you; most of the Iraqi people are thankful to the American troops who liberated our country and apprehended that lunatic Saddam, but, as you know, everything has vices and virtues, and this war is not exempted. The good thing is that the former regime's grip on Iraq is lost and unclenched, and that regime is now a part of history . . . But there's a main problem that should be overcome. Security. big word . . . ha! You see, it's very likely to see rebellion down the streets here because of the security-absence conditions . . . it makes us feel disappointed somehow.

. . . Are you satisfied now? You should know that we thank the American soldiers who left their homeland and came down here to help and free us, but don't think that we're weak or cowards. On the contrary, we're a strong nation and as soon as we get our sovereignty and become democratic and free, then we'll be able to protect our oil and country by ourselves because we're a very great nation which is one of the most ancient civilizations that participated in the building and development of the world.

Now I think that's enough.

I wish that this friendship lasts for good, hopefully that we meet someday (who knows . . . it's a small world).

Farewell,
Sincerely
Haider

8

FARIS: FRIEND AND TRANSLATOR

Sprinkled throughout Iraq, more numerously in Baghdad, are scores of unsung and unknown heroes. Mostly young men and women, these are Iraqis who have risked and, in some cases, given their lives to bridge the gap between worlds colliding in their native country.

Some work for the occupying military and foreign contractors, pulling down top dollar and exposing themselves to great risk. Some have quit those positions out of fear of reprisal; some have refused those lucrative stations because of conscience pangs, deciding instead to take up the crucial work of translating for one of the NGOs (nongovernmental organizations) working in Iraq such as CARE or perhaps for the corporate press. The risk for these translators is only slightly less.

And then there are the brave, sometimes idealistic, sometimes simply unemployed Iraqis who work with the ragtag independents—journalists, human rights workers, and peace groups—who have very small, unreliable budgets, no corporate expense accounts, and frequently want to go to the most dangerous and out-of-the-way places.

I had the good fortune to meet one of the latter types of translators and we hit it off well enough that he agreed to continue driving and translating during my weeks in his country. Faris (whose last name will go unstated for obvious reasons) was not only an excellent translator, his insights into Iraqi life and culture helped enormously. We rode many dusty miles in his well-worn, nondescript Buick Opel.

He would probably be offended that I call his car a "rattletrap," but I do so with the greatest affection and respect. Traveling in Faris's rattletrap was safer than riding in any shiny, new SUV bristling with armed guards. In fact, we began calling those oversized gas hogs "SMVs" for "Shoot Me Vehicles," as a way of describing how natural a target they became, and considered ourselves much better protected by "swimming with the fish."

Faris was trained as an engineer and had served his mandatory eighteen months in the Iraqi Army under Saddam Hussein. He lived with his widowed mother in what was once a middle-class section of Baghdad, keeping his father's small lathe and machine tools in a special room.

One day I asked him to write his thoughts about his life and his country in its terribly turbulent moment of history. Proud of his ability to write as well as speak English, he refused to pen his statement in Arabic.

I am a young man has borne in Iraq in 1971 and I have never traveled abroad. The most regular access for me to know what is going on outside is the BBC. I hate politics as much as my daddy liked it. I would like to write some ideas about our life in the presence of the occupation.

The situation in Iraq has become worse but it is expected to be worst. In the present time, military jets are bombing the pockets of terrorists as commonly said by the US announcers. The attacks between both sides is becoming more sever like using heavy artillery by the resistance to bomb the CPA (Saddam former presidential palace) and other US army camps and baises and police stations. Sideways bombs are now the weapons of random destruction.

Baghdad city is now used as a combat area paying no attention to the lives of civilians. I think that we should leave the city for them in order to fight and go out of Baghdad to the rural areas to live where we can find more security with no big difference with what relates to the civil services like electricity, water, fuel, hospitals and sewage, etc. At least we can solve the traffic jam problem!

A remarkable note is to say that the media has stopped covering all the explosions inside Baghdad and the international public starts to think that they are really stopped. But this is wrong and I think that the media is now considered as one of the terrorist pockets which should be defeated because reporting about any resistance action is now considered as a participation and support for terrorism.

The objective of this campaign is still a big mystery more than the weapons of mass deception itself. For me I call it "Toppling Saddam's Regime" campaign because this is the only achievement yet. But there are many important and controversial questions that arise for our future.

Are we Iraqis now or something else? Is it part of the new democracy in Iraq to make us forget all about our nationality? Are our nation supposed to forget every thing about our culture and heritage so that we can forget Sadam then? Is this a freedom campaign or is it a new version of imperialism which tries to disfigure our nation and make us look like them? For sure they are controlling our future but are they willing and trying to change our history, too?

President Bush have said, "Either you are with us or with the terrorists" and I would like to tell him that we are neither with the terrorists nor with him. We still have ethics that forbid us from joining both of you!

Baghdad, Iraq
16 Feb. 2004

9

DEMOCRACY, DICTATORS, AND THE FATE OF WIDAD SHWAISH

"Is this the democracy of civilized people in the U.S., to kill innocent human beings with no reason? Those soldiers represent U.S. people. I can't say that U.S. people are bad, but they accuse others of having dictatorships when they are the ones that have dictators."

With that irate indictment, Sheik Khalid Hussain unburdened some of the pain and resentment he felt from living in occupied Iraq, from hearing too many tales of people killed by U.S. troops, and from being held for three weeks in an open field surrounded by razor wire, without shelter or sanitation.

In late November 2003, Sheik Hussain was detained with fifteen other men and held for twenty-one days at the Army's Fourth Infantry Division base near Balad, about forty miles north of Baghdad. For the first five days this man, responsible for 1,500 people of the Albousihail tribe, said he and his fellow detainees lived in the open, and received blankets only as other detainees were released. During one three-day period of their detention, he said it rained continually and blankets were their only shelter.

Asked what he was charged with, the Sheik responded that an Army interpreter told him, "You don't cooperate with coalition forces. You don't give us names of terrorists." He said he and others were accused of supporting the mujahadin (resistance fighters) but said they have since been cleared of those accusations and released after what he called a "deal with (Lt. Col.) Sassaman" that there would be no more attacks from inside the wire at Abu Hishma. He claimed that "if Colonel Sassaman knows you're talking with me, he'll send his troops to detain me again."

Helping the U.S. military find civil defense workers is something Sheik Hussain saw as part of his job. "I gave the coalition forces 10 names of people who could do civil defense work," such as guarding the checkpoint into the village. But now he is clearly angry when talking about the troops occupying his country.

"Now that Saddam Hussein is captured, what's the reason to keep scaring people, to describe anyone who defends their country as a terrorist? If we occupied the U.S., wouldn't you defend your country?"

"We are simple people and farmers, but the U.S. will be defeated like in Vietnam, this time by the Iraqi people. If Americans knew the real number of U.S. troops killed in Iraq they would rebel against the government. Why don't the mass media report the truth? We hear on satellite news that over ten U.S. soldiers have been killed in the last few days. For us, we don't like U.S. people to be killed. We are sorry for their deaths. We are farmers. We are farmers."

As much as Sheik Hussain's remarks were angry and animated, the next person's words were distant and detached. Standing outside his brother Shamar's home, Saddam Shwaish retold with a few hollow words how his sister-in-law was killed the night of October 16, 2003.

At 9:30 that night, Shwaish said, U.S. troops were on patrol southeast of the village of Abu Hishma, advancing toward where we stood. Widad, Shamar's wife, aged 27, went outside to get some water. Within fifty feet of the back door, clearly in sight of where we stood, several soldiers hid in the tall, green cotton plants. Without warning, a shot rang out, hitting Widad in the neck and killing her. She was the mother of five children, aged six months to twelve years. Her husband Shamar continues to serve as the primary school principal in Balad.

In trying to get a response from the U.S. military, I attempted without success to contact by email two PAOs (Public Affairs Officers) from the Army's 4th Infantry Division for comment. One message bounced back from a "full inbox." The other was answered by an officer responding that he had been reassigned to Germany. Finally, during my visit to Sassaman's battalion of the 4th Infantry Division, I was able to question someone who had knowledge of how Widad Shwaish died.

Lieutenant Colonel Nathan Sassaman gave me a brief description of the Iraqi woman's death, saying "Shwaish was killed with a small-caliber handgun." There was an "action nearby" (firefight between his troops and Iraqis) that night during which the Army returned fire, "but we fired no handguns, so U.S. troops could not have caused Shwaish's death."

"We were in an action," Sassaman concluded. "It probably makes sense for the Iraqis to blame her death on the Americans. I'd probably have done the same thing."

The battalion's Executive Officer, Major Rob Gwinner, was responsible for the follow-up investigation done with the Iraqi Police. The next day I spoke with the Major, whose account of the Shwaish shooting was predictably poles apart from the account I got from her relatives.

Gwinner said that when Shwaish was shot, U.S. troops were at a location such that it would have been impossible for her to have been shot by them. He said that an Iraqi doctor he spoke with refused to let him see Shwaish's body or see the bullet that killed her, asking instead for a few dollars' compensation to aid the dead woman's children. To this career officer, packing his bags to leave Iraq with his battalion after a year's tour of duty, all this was simply further proof that Widad Shwaish was not killed by U.S. troops.

I started to press Gwinner with a final question from the Iraqis' perspective but stopped when I remembered his response to an earlier one: "It's not that we're cynical," he said with a smile, "it's just that they're all pathological liars."

10

ON THEIR WAY TO ABU GHRAIB

"How could this happen?" nearly everyone asked as photos poured forth from Abu Ghraib showing American soldiers torturing Iraqi prisoners. But even as the United States finally released a few hundred of the more than 10,000 men locked up in that prison, another question, "Why were so many Iraqis detained in the first place?" needs to be asked.

The story of what happened at the farming hamlet of Abu Siffa, forty miles north of Baghdad, explains a lot.

"On December 16, 2003, at 2:00 A.M, on a rainy night, all the houses in Abu Siffa, about two dozen, were surrounded by U.S. troops in tanks and humvees. They surrounded the fields of the farmers by tanks and they destroyed the fences of the fields," citrus farmer, Mohammed Al-Tai explained to a delegation from CPT visiting the village to document detainees' stories.

Soldiers from the Army's 4th Infantry Division rounded up two attorneys, fifteen schoolteachers, men in their eighties, a blind man, police officers, young teens, and an elderly man so frail he had to be carried by the soldiers, Al-Tai said. In all, eighty-three men disappeared that night, virtually every male in the village.

His description of that night continued. "They destroyed the doors of the houses and of the rooms. At night usually the doors of the bedrooms are locked, so they kicked the doors in and destroyed them by their weapons. After that they gathered the men, beating them severely. One was an old man and they smashed his glasses, and for that old man they had to guide him."

Before the soldiers finished the Abu Siffa raid, Al-Tai added that they also "stole from Imad, the attorney, about 14 million dinars ($10,370). From his father, Kamel, they stole 4.5 million dinars ($3,300). They stole 4 million dinars ($3000) from Ziad, an Iraqi police officer, and from all the other houses together, about 100,000 to 150,000 dinars ($75 to $110). They also took five cars. Later they returned two of them that belonged to police officers who died in the line of duty."

A local farmer took us on a tour of this village's citrus groves, stuffing our pockets full of oranges and grapefruit. Pictured with him is Christian Peacemaker Team member, Stewart Vriesinga. Behind them, in the jacket, is Jim Loney, one of the four CPT members taken hostage in November, 2005. (*Photo by Mike Ferner*)

The reason for the raid was to apprehend Kais Hattam, Al-Tai said, adding that Hattam claimed he planned to surrender to the Americans the following morning. Later in an interview, Lieutenant Colonel Nathan Sassaman, commander of the division's 1st Battalion, the unit responsible for the district including Abu Siffa, confirmed that Hattam was their man, but doubted he would have surrendered voluntarily.

Sassaman said that Hattam was on a "wanted" list because his name appeared in Ba'ath Party documents found with Saddam Hussein, captured less than three days before the Abu Siffa raid. He described Hattam as a "key figure, one of five regional directors of the Ba'ath Party."

The Lieutenant Colonel's version of the raid was that seventy-three people, not eighty-three, were rounded up, all adults. He said his men found a several-acre compound with a large quantity of material for making IEDs (Improvised Explosive Devices), weapons, and "just a ton of explosives." He added that three of the detainees were later released for health reasons.

Asked why so many villagers were rounded up after the Army got the man they were looking for, he replied that the amount of weapons and explosives implicated Abu Siffa as a center of resistance, further proven by the fact that his base had been mortared from that area.

The CPT delegation in Abu Siffa listened to Mohammed Al-Tai and several of his neighbors explain that six weeks after the December predawn

On the night of January 2, 2004, soldiers returned to Abu Siffa and destroyed this house in response to a mortar attack earlier that day that took the life of Captain Eric Paliwoda from the 1st Battalion. (*Photo by Mike Ferner*)

raid on their village, seventy-nine adult men were still held in Abu Ghraib, still without visiting privileges. They said that one ill detainee had been released. Contrary to Sassaman's claim that no children were apprehended, Al-Tai said three children had been transferred to Al-Karkh, a special youth prison in Baghdad, which the farmer and another villager said they'd been able to visit, albeit under difficult conditions. "It is not easy to get there, the lines are very long, and even family members are kept behind a line twenty feet away from their children."

Hania, wife of attorney-detainee, Kamel Khoumais, added in sad tones, "For forty-seven days I did not see him. I tried. I went to Abu Ghraib prison twice. I was turned back with tears." On the night of the raid, soldiers took their family car, she related, and her little finger, still swollen and red, was broken when the keys were ripped out of her hand.

The raid that swept up all of Abu Siffa's men is only part of that village's story.

After describing the December 16 roundup, Al-Tai took the delegation on a door-to-door tour of his village, starting with a vacant house where Abbas Abdwahid had lived with fifteen members of his extended family. The 41-year-old primary school teacher and several other former residents of the home were now in Abu Ghraib. Large holes in the brick walls, daylight through the roof, and an orange and white VW Passat taxi smashed up against a rear corner of the house by a Bradley Fighting Vehicle were silent reminders of the Army's second raid on Abu Siffa, on New Year's Eve.

No men were apprehended this time, Al-Tai said; "there were none left." The purpose of the return visit was made clear when the Bradley gunners opened fire with the 25 mm Bushmaster chain gun and the 7.62 mm machine gun, blasting holes large and small into the brick and cement-block home.

On January 2, the military came back. Al-Tai showed us the rear of another vacant house where he said four brothers, now all in Abu Ghraib, once lived. Still visible were the tracks the Bradley made as it approached the home of Hamis, Abd Kadir, Mohammed, and Jasim. As with the previous raid, there was no resistance, Al-Tai said. After another display of firepower the soldiers left. The uninhabitable home, a flattened brick outhouse, a pile of 25 mm shell casings, and a steel door shot off its hinges, bleeding rust stains from dozens of bullet holes, spoke of that night's violence. As the CPT delegation listened, one of the villagers added, "The soldiers warned the people that they will make this area 'just like the land of the moon . . . it will not be good to plant . . . it will be like the desert.'"

When asked why the Army returned twice to destroy homes, the 1st Battalion's Executive Officer, Major Rob Gwinner, countered the homes were "still habitable. People are living in them." His boss, Lieutenant Colonel Sassaman, said the subsequent raids were a reaction to mortar attacks against his base from the Abu Siffa area. Pentagon casualty reports state that on January 2, 28-year-old Captain Eric Paliwoda was killed in a mortar attack at the 1st Battalion's base.

The prisoner abuse at Abu Ghraib provides the public with a painful education on the Geneva Conventions' proscription of torture. To that lesson we can add the story of how people were rounded up and homes destroyed in places like Abu Siffa—further violations of the Conventions' prohibition against "collective penalties."

11

INSIDE THE WIRE AT ABU HISHMA

In a rented minivan stuffed full of CPT members, I arrive at the farming town of Abu Hishma, ten minutes before the 5:00 P.M. curfew imposed by the U.S. Army. The curfew as well as several miles of razor wire that encircle the small town are the army's response to an RPG attack by resistance fighters near here that took the life of Sergeant Dale Panchot.

Inside the wire, kids of all ages spill into the narrow dirt streets from every direction, smiling, laughing, and waving. Barely more than a lane, the road is still muddy from earlier rains. Bouncing along, the minivan lurches perilously close to the ditch when oncoming vehicles approach. Each time we turn a corner, it appears certain we will run over one of the kids or at least send somebody tumbling into the ditch, but somehow they dart from harm's way. Running after the van, they shout "Saddam! Saddam!" but it's not clear how much of the shouting is a political statement and how much of it is kids being kids for a rare carload of foreigners.

Our contact, a local journalist, is nowhere to be found. We are creeping along with a boisterous bunch in tow, moments before curfew, not sure if we have a place to stay for the night. The driver offers the hospitality of his home to seven strangers as a last resort. The CPT members decide to call on the local sheik responsible for the welfare of about 25,000 residents of Abu Hishma, some inside and some outside the wire.

The sheik's oldest son, Shalon, welcomes us warmly. His English, learned while studying Recent U.S. History at the University of Baghdad, is quite good. Soon his father arrives. We discuss the issues of the day in Abu Hishma, and without warning, our second chicken-and-rice dinner of the evening is served by two youngsters. Barely two hours earlier, in the nearby village of Abu Siffa, we had eaten a similar feast at the home of another farmer.

After eating, drinking tea, and further discussion, the same youngsters who served and cleared away the meal bring in fabric mats and blankets for bedtime. The sheik makes sure each guest is comfortable, leans his AK-47 against the wall next to his pillow, and retires.

The next day begins early, and we are soon on our way to see more of this small town fifty miles north of Baghdad.

This typical Iraqi farming village is unlike any I've seen in the United States, where farmhouses are always widely scattered, single-family homes with accompanying barns and outbuildings—the typical white frame house and red barn—surrounded by enough lawn to require a miniature tractor.

Here, the landscape is completely different, and not just because of the dry climate. The homes are tiny by comparison. A few have postage stamp-sized yards but, in most cases, lawns are replaced by barnyards—meaning that the chickens, goats, cows, manure piles, and mud-hut outbuildings are literally a few steps from the door. Mixed in with the animals and sheds are bundles of neatly stacked fruit tree prunings, piles of harvested cotton stalks, and other material ready for the stove. The dirt lanes are bordered by rounded, earthen walls about four feet tall. Colorful blankets air on second-story balconies.

Soon the muddy lanes become more than the heavily loaded van can navigate, so we get out and walk. The kids mug for our cameras, running and jumping in front of, alongside, and behind us. Some wear light jackets against the chilly morning air. Most are barefoot, oblivious to several varieties of manure dotting the trail.

Ahead on the left is the first stop on our Abu Hishma walking tour: the foundation of a house that perfectly frames a bomb crater fifteen feet deep and thirty feet wide. Miraculously, the family of seven was gone when an air strike turned their house into another product of what the *Glossary of Military Terms & Slang from the Vietnam War* refers to as "H & I," or harassment and interdiction fire: "Random artillery (or aerial) bombardments used to deny the enemy terrain which they might find beneficial to their campaign; general rather than specific, confirmed military targets." Or, depending on your perspective, a random terror strike.

Local kids show us some other effects of the blast, including one of their pals, Hamed, who wears a gauze patch taped over a missing right eye taken out by bomb shrapnel. Two boys poke a stick at an orange and white cat that has achieved immortality for having been killed by the bomb. We're shown window frames in homes two blocks away where cardboard replaces the glass reportedly shattered by the same explosion.

A hundred feet up the lane, a smaller bomb crater is off to the side. But before we hear its story, we're distracted by the roar of six U.S. helicopter gunships darting low overhead.

We return to the cars and drive a short distance to our next stop, a slightly larger farmhouse on the edge of the village. It is the home of Yaseen, a

33 year-old farmer who attended evening classes at the University of Baghdad's Islamic Studies program and who, according to his uncle, Muhnna, was detained by U.S. soldiers and jailed in Abu Ghraib. Months later, the uncle said, he learned from prisoners released from that infamous facility that Yaseen, still unable to see visitors, was charged with "terrorist acts."

Just then, two U.S. helicopters fly low over the village, circle, and fire machine gun bursts into an open pasture a couple of hundred meters away. "They do it just to scare us," one villager shrugs. When I mentioned this to a former Iraqi soldier, he replied, "Yes, we used to call it 'showing the teeth.'"

A rooster crows in Yaseen's farmyard. Chickens scratch in a small, neatly fenced front yard. In the dirty side yard are two red heifers, an earthen oven, a mud brick outhouse and piles of stacked brush. Several small Holstein dairy cows graze in a narrow, rich pasture just beyond the lane. Muhnna says with equal parts disappointment and anger in his voice, "Soldiers that do these kinds of things don't deserve to be called Americans." Two more helicopters roar in from another direction. They circle a few hundred meters to the west and go on their way.

◆ ◆ ◆

A couple of weeks later, I run into a couple of CPT members on Karrada Street in Baghdad, and learn that there's been another incident in Abu Hishma. This time, two sheiks have taken the unusual step to travel to Baghdad to personally ask the CPT's assistance.

The sheiks said that two days earlier, two young men from the village were shot and killed by U.S. troops. The Iraqis say the men were innocent, killed as they walked down the road. (The Army later refutes that claim, saying they were killed as they planted rockets for a later attack on the base outside Abu Hishma.) The next day finds me once again on the dusty road north out of Baghdad with several CPT members.

Arriving in Abu Hishma, we are greeted by an enormous tent with green stripes and red and purple floral designs, set up alongside one of the irrigation canals on the edge of the village. Well over 100 males, from kids to elders, sit on chairs or the carpeted ground under the tent, attending a funeral wake for a sheik's son. He was killed the day before, villagers tell us, by gunfire from a U.S. helicopter as he drove back from the funeral for the two young men killed alongside the road. Later that day, villagers show us the pickup truck the sheik's son was driving when he was killed. A single hole indicates where a bullet entered the cab to the rear of the driver, exiting through the back of the small, worn bench seat now covered with a large blood stain. That a helicopter gunship attack would leave only one bullet hole seems questionable, and I place this incident into my growing file of "grey stories."

Inside the tent, however, the wake is underway and we are invited to sit down. A pack of cigarettes each is placed on the low table before us, a youth brings a pitcher of water and some soap for hand-washing, and we are asked to join in a meal of lamb stewed in tomatoes over rice. At a time of grieving for a young man said to have been killed by the American military, we are the guests of honor. We eat first and over 100 people wait for us to finish before anyone else is served.

After we eat and pay our respects to the sheik, a young boy asks if we want to see "where the cruise missile hit two days ago?" Throwing the rest of the day's schedule to the wind, we follow him down a narrow lane bordered by small farming plots, orchards, and homes. Before long, we see the edge of a postage stamp-sized orange grove, beyond which are a few twisted, blackened orange trees and an enormous hole in the ground.

Kids gather from neighboring farms, talking excitedly in Arabic and pointing to the remnants of orange grove and the massive hole. Through our interpreter I ask a couple of them if they can find any shrapnel, and watch as they scramble down the sides of the fifteen-foot crater, returning with several pieces of twisted steel.

The farmer whose grove it was appears in a gray dishdasha, speaking quietly and occasionally smiling. At one point, Cliff Kindy, who operates a small farm in Indiana, introduces himself to Abu Kalaf, explaining that he also farms back home, and asks a stunningly frank joke of a question. "What

Windows in this village were blown out by what residents said was a nighttime cruise missile strike that destroyed a farmer's portion of Abu Hishma's collective orange grove. (*Photo by Mike Ferner*)

kind of crops do you grow in your crater?" Kalaf appreciates Cliff's grim wit, laughs, and invites us in for a cup of tea.

At the end of a very long day, I suspend taking notes to enjoy the hot, sweet brew and take a few pictures of the children who have come inside. Giggles erupt immediately behind me and I turn, taking a quick photo of a beautiful child framed by some steel grating—all that's left in the window frame when the missile blew up the orange grove two nights earlier.

12

TWO MYSTERIOUS DEATHS AND THE INCIDENT NEAR RAMADI

Two of the stories I covered in Iraq were exceedingly frustrating because they remained so unresolved, but they ultimately taught me an important lesson about trying to discern the truth in a place like Iraq.

The first was the story of a young Iraqi man and woman in the Taha family, who were shot and killed by U.S. troops along the edge of their small farming town of Abu Hishma, near the city of Balad, about forty miles north of Baghdad. While in Iraq in 2004, I filed a piece about the incident that ran on some Internet sites under the title, "The Countryside Murders."

That story was based on information I got from two relatives of the people who were killed, who said they were eyewitnesses to what happened. This is how they reported those events to me.

One day in October 2003, Aziz Taha was shot and killed by soldiers "firing randomly" as they patrolled beyond their base at a former Iraqi airfield three kilometers south of the Taha home, according to Muhnna Azazzal, Aziz Taha's uncle. Taha, who was also a fourth-year student at the University of Baghdad's English Studies Department, was shot during the random shooting and fell, mortally wounded.

Aziz Taha's sister-in-law, Majida, saw him fall and rushed to his aid. Struck by another bullet, she died instantly, leaving behind three children, the youngest only fifteen days old.

During the two hours Azazzal said his nephew lay dying, U.S. troops surrounded the scene and kept the neighbors back, preventing first aid from reaching the wounded man.

Taha's sister, Asmaa, said that she witnessed the shootings and began to cry hysterically when she saw her brother, Aziz, shot and bleeding to death. She said that an American soldier responded to her cries by firing his rifle into the ground near Aziz's dying body "to mock my grief."

That was the story I recounted in "The Countryside Murders."

Weeks later, when I visited the Army's 4th Infantry Division at Forward Operations Base (FOB) Paliwoda, near Balad, I got a markedly different story from Battalion Commander, Lieutenant Colonel Nathan Sassaman. In response to my questions about the shooting deaths of Aziz and Majida Taha, Sassaman recalled events this way.

Aziz Taha was on a list of suspects to be detained. As a unit of his battalion was in the process of doing so, "a sniper opened fire on my men, wounding one in the arm, and Taha escaped," Sassaman said. "We returned fire and Majida was caught in the crossfire."

Taha was shot and fell, Sassaman said, and "We began aid when I arrived about 30 minutes or so later."

The Lieutenant Colonel said he assumed that Majida's neighbors took her to the hospital, but when he later went to the Taha home, he found Majida lying dead in the front yard. He added that his soldiers "found lots of weapons in Aziz's home."

During the two days and nights I stayed at FOB Paliwoda, I spoke with Sassaman and his executive officer (XO), Major Rob Gwinner, about this and other incidents in which I'd been told that Iraqis were shot and/or had their homes destroyed by their battalion's troops. In addition to getting vastly different stories from what Iraqis told me, I was even more surprised at how sketchy, if any, the official records were of such incidents.

Gwinner said, and Sassaman confirmed, that the Battalion's daily logbook would have showed only the briefest of entries for the Taha shootings, basically the map coordinates and the fact that a soldier had been wounded in an exchange of gunfire. When asked what other records were available, Gwinner said that he kept more detailed accounts of such incidents in his "day planner" but had already taken those pages out and sent them back home to Ft. Carson, Colorado.

The second story, about an incident near Ramadi on November 22, 2003, was one I dug into much further, but by the time I had to leave Iraq I felt no closer to the truth.

Several people who claimed to be eyewitnesses to this incident related a horrific account of what they described as an Army house raid gone terribly bad in the tiny village of al-Jazeera, outside Ramadi, about seventy miles west of Baghdad.

During the shootout, according to witnesses, four U.S. troops killed each other in a "friendly fire" episode. In revenge, the remaining soldiers summarily executed three Iraqi detainees, hit a pickup truck with five other civilians in it with tank fire, killing all aboard, and called in an air strike to destroy the family's home.

Again, the Army's version was poles apart from what the Iraqis told me. But compounding the difficulty in finding the truth were the local forensic examiner who spoke in riddles and an attorney who initially was very helpful but succumbed to a severe case of cold feet.

In mid-February, 2004 almost three months after the incident happened, I visited al-Jazeera with the CPT and interviewed surviving members of the family and the attorney who represented them in an effort to get compensation. At that time, the attorney gave me his statement on the record.

That same day I listened to a young woman describe in detail how she watched U.S. troops carry four dead soldiers, killed by their own comrades, out of her home; how soldiers ordered two of her brothers and her brother-in-law out of the house, told them to lay face down on the ground, and shot them as she watched.

She also explained how five neighbors in a pickup truck who had just left the nearby mosque, drove by the village to see what was happening and were fired on and killed by a U.S. tank; how soldiers began shelling and shooting at the house, and how "also they used airplanes and helicopter to bomb the house."

The house she referred to was little more than a pile of rubble. Family members and neighbors scavenged stones from it to rebuild on a new foundation. Next to the destroyed home stood another, thoroughly riddled with holes and pockmarks from large and small caliber guns. In the garage, a white Toyota sedan sat immobilized with over a dozen bullet holes in it.

Ten days later, I returned to al-Jazeera to get more information. Faris arranged a driver and we took the Baghdad Airport highway out of town, past Abu Ghraib prison, past Fallujah, exiting at Ramadi. With no phone service in Iraq to call and set up a meeting, our first stop was at the Ramadi courthouse to look for the lawyer representing the survivors. Attorneys and clients milled about, some waiting for hearings, others looking for their names on a short list of people who had won compensation from the U.S. military.

We stayed only long enough to speak with a member of the Iraq Human Rights Organization, a colleague of the lawyer we were looking for, who told us he was not in. In those few minutes, word circulated that an American *sahife* was writing a story about people killed in a raid outside of town. Attorneys pressed in, asking, demanding that we look into their cases as well. "Here, this one happened just last week! Why do you want to investigate an old story . . . Let me tell you about this one . . . Look, coalition forces killed this man's brother and father . . . "

Never before had I been in a situation where people started grabbing my arm and my shirt with such hope and desperation on their faces. I started to reply, "I'm sorry, but I can't help you . . . I can't help you . . . I can't . . . " My gut wrenched. Faris caught my eye with a look that said, "Let's go."

After a quick exit from the courthouse, we decided to call on the forensic examiner at the Ramadi hospital.

Earlier, CPT members told me that when they first came to investigate the incident a week after it happened, he was unavailable. Others they spoke with, however, claimed that the official cause of death in such incidents was always noted as shrapnel, never bullets. Such a practice clouded the record, making it impossible in some situations to determine how someone died. With that in mind, I was determined to find the examiner and ask him some very direct questions.

We were lucky. Dr. Hamdi, Chief of Forensics, Ramadi General Hospital, was in his office and willing to talk.

I explained the reason for our visit: to find out the truth about how the three men died on November 22, 2003. "I would like to find out the truth, too," Dr. Hamdi responded, raising my hopes.

He reviewed the summary log with us from the date of the incident, saying that he could not show us the full reports without a court order. But after a few minutes, he sent an assistant to get the full reports.

The assistant came back with an oversized volume and Dr. Hamdi read his report of one of the victims, Ibrahim Ahmed, prepared at 4:00 P.M. on November 23, 2003. The report was divided into descriptions of the outside and inside anatomy.

Dr. Hamdi read that Ahmed's body had "tears of different shapes on the left shoulder, right neck, left arm, upper right arm, chest, abdomen, and both legs. From the shapes of the tears they were caused by shell pieces. Inside, there was bleeding in the chest cavity, broken ribs, tears in the lungs, tears in the bowel. No shells found in the body."

I asked Dr. Hamdi if Ibrahim Ahmed had been shot . . . if there were any bullets found in the body. The Chief of Forensics replied only that the body had been "affected by shells."

Children from the village of Al-Jazeera, where the "Incident Near Ramadi" happened. (*Photo by Mike Ferner*)

I pressed him twice more to explain what that meant. "Does that mean he was shot?" Each time the doctor responded by saying only that "the body had been affected by shells."

Next, I asked him if anyone from the U.S. military had spoken with him about this case. He replied, "No." However, another man sitting in the small office smiled slightly and nodded his head, "yes." Unfortunately the other man left before we finished talking with Dr. Hamdi and I couldn't ask him to confirm what he had indicated.

Dr. Hamdi then looked at Faris and said, "I can tell what this person died from, but I will only tell a judge in court."

He then returned to the forensic reports and noted that the second victim had been examined at 11:00 A.M. on November 23, 2003, by a Dr. Katan. Hamdi repeated that he was not supposed to show us the full reports without a court order, and clearly wanted to end the interview.

After negotiating with the driver for an additional fee to travel back to al-Jazeera, we went once more to the village to speak with the attorney. At the outset, he insisted that I could not use his name in what I wrote. He explained that when he began representing the families of the three men who had been killed in this incident, all his cases in that court were "marked and delayed." He said word was getting around that he was representing "terrorists," and that he did not want to risk further notoriety by being in a story.

When I explained our conversation with Dr. Hamdi, the attorney replied that he had filed a complaint against Dr. Hamdi with the Ministry of Health, and a complaint with a judge at the court in Ramadi, claiming that "this doctor is working under influence of Coalition Forces. If he mentions the truth, Coalition Forces will be convicted."

I asked him how he knew that Dr. Hamdi was being pressured, and he replied, "There are many clues; not just this case. All his reports say the same thing, that the body was 'affected by shells' even if the body has been badly burned."

Going back to the killings in his village, he added that the "second day (after the incident) soldiers came back to search for evidence, for an excuse for the raid. They began to demolish the house. They found no evidence. So soldiers went to the nearby mosque to apologize" to one of the clerics.

The mother of one of the victims came out to where we stood on the windswept rise overlooking the bombed house. I asked her if she wanted to add anything about what happened on the night of the raid. She replied, "After Coalition Forces executed the three men, they took their bodies across the road. Two soldiers offered us food. Two other soldiers came over to the women and children and they wanted to kill all of us, but two 'red ones' (red-haired soldiers) stopped them."

Running out of time and money to hire drivers and translators, I was intent on returning once more to Ramadi before leaving Iraq. The attorney in al-Jazeera had told me about an Army captain he had met with in his attempts to get compensation for the family of the three men killed in the

November incident. Faris arranged another trip so we could meet with Captain Mark Stamper of the 1st Infantry Division.

Outside the Ramadi Directorate (municipal area) building, long lines of people filed past armed U.S. soldiers to present their claims and make inquiries about missing relatives. After introducing myself to one of the GIs, he took us inside past dozens of waiting Iraqis, to a tiny office where Captain Stamper and a translator sat behind a small desk.

I introduced myself and explained why I was there. Stamper's first remark was that he was familiar with the facts of the case because just three days before he had met with the family's attorney and the mother we spoke with in al-Jazeera. Then he hurried to state, "We're not going to be an insurance claim company for bad guys here," he began. "We can't pay out any compensation in this case because it resulted from a combat incident."

I told him that was not the impression I got from interviewing witnesses and he replied, "Look. There are some legitimate stories here," and described the case of an Iraqi who was killed when an IED (improvised explosive device) blew up alongside a U.S. convoy. He awarded compensation to the surviving family members. "We don't have any requirement to do any of this, really. We basically do it to establish friendship and good relations."

About the November 22 incident at Al-Jazeera, Stamper said that U.S. troops had been fired on first, when "someone threw a grenade . . . there was NO friendly fire incident. Two teams never come in from opposite sides of a building at the same time, to prevent that very kind of problem."

Asked how the three Iraqi men were killed, he denied they were executed. "We are fighting a war of insurgency here. We need information. Why would we kill people we could get information from? That's why this story smells of fabrication. We had no reason to kill these men. They were worth more to us alive than dead."

He said they had targeted this house in the first place because the Army got information that insurgents used it. He said that following the raid, they found weapons, "about 20 RPGs," and a suicide note that looked like it was written for a potential suicide bomber, a copy of which he said he gave to the family's attorney.

I asked if he had any photographic evidence of weapons and suicide notes. He said he did, but didn't have immediate access to it. Echoing Lieutenant Colonel Sassaman's earlier claim about record keeping, Stamper said that no formal report was made on the incident.

About the villagers' claim that U.S. soldiers returned after the raid and verbally apologized to a cleric at the mosque, he smiled and said, "They say this all the time—that we made an apology. We didn't apologize. We got the bad guys."

Next stop after lunch in Ramadi was a final ride to al-Jazeera to talk with the attorney. After waiting over an hour for him, our driver began to get worried that we would be on the road back after dark, something neither he nor Faris recommended.

While we hung around the car and waited, the mother came out of her house to visit. I asked her more questions about the November incident, including Stamper's claim that troops had found a large quantity of weapons when they searched the demolished house. She recalled that the day after the incident, troops returned to search houses and in one nearby home found a store of Kalashnikovs. The owner of them, however, was a former Iraqi police officer who was responsible for maintaining weapons and had the necessary books and inventory records, so he was not detained. She concluded by saying that when she met with Stamper in Ramadi several days earlier, she had spoken with the captain's Lebanese translator, who told her that Stamper said troops had given a verbal apology to villagers and admitted they had the wrong house.

Just as I was about to give in to the driver's appeals to get underway, the attorney appeared.

One of the reasons I wanted to see the attorney before I left was to get copies of Dr. Hamdi's full reports on each of the three dead men, which the attorney had said he would get a judge's order to release. But without any excuse, he simply said he did not have them.

His next remark struck me as very strange, indeed. He asked me to informally intervene with Stamper, "You know, American to American," on his behalf and on behalf of the family to try to get compensation for them.

I told him that was just not something a journalist could do. Disappointed and frustrated, and with the driver demanding we get going, I said goodbye to the attorney and the mother. With a final look at the tiny village of al-Jazeera, now cloaked in even more mystery, we drove away.

On the way back to Baghdad, realizing that within thirty-six hours I would be leaving Iraq for perhaps the last time and feeling quite the failure in this case, I hoped for some comforting words from the usually witty Faris. Instead, he expressed with rare emotion and disdain, his displeasure with the attorney, saying, "All he's interested in is compensation. Why not justice? The compensation he'll get for the family at most will be $1,000. That's how much a cow costs. Do he and the family think the lives of their sons are worth only a cow? They should forget the compensation and go for justice to convict the soldiers responsible for this."

"True . . . true," I thought to myself in the back seat. Then images came to mind of impoverished villagers trying to exact even a thousand dollars from the most powerful military on earth and I wondered if the truth would ever come out about the incident near Ramadi, or justice for its alleged victims.

PART III

ACTIVISTS, JOURNALISTS, SOLDIERS, AND CLOWNS

13

COURAGE UNDER FIRE

There are few people, especially American citizens, who can say they voluntarily traveled to Iraq and put their lives on the line trying to stop a war. Kathy Kelly can. Not once, but twice.

In 1991, this diminutive Irish-American from Chicago's South Side joined the "Gulf Peace Team," comprising seventy-two activists from eighteen nations, to literally sit down in the desert on the Iraq–Saudi border near Kuwait. Initially, they witnessed an air war from their desert encampment, feeling dismayed and irrelevant as warplanes regularly flew overhead. Iraqi authorities evacuated the team to Baghdad just before Bush the Elder's troops began the brief, horrific ground war phase of the Gulf War. Nevertheless, the peace team's effort was historic.

Fast-forward to April 2003. With Saddam Hussein's palaces still smoking across the Tigris River, young U.S. Marines stopped their tanks in front of the Al-Fanar Hotel and were greeted by three American peace activists who had endured weeks of "shock and awe" bombing. A sergeant who gratefully accepted the oranges, dates, and bottled water offered by the women, said in stunning understatement, "This here's a pretty dangerous place for you to be, ma'am." "We know," Kathy Kelly replied. "It's been pretty dangerous the last three weeks you've been bombing us, too."

What would compel a middle-aged schoolteacher with a Master's degree in Religious Education to twice place herself in the course of an invading U.S. army?

The singlemindedness and tenacity that drove her work on behalf of the people of Iraq does not surprise those who knew the petite redhead as a high-school teacher in the 1970s. The Chicago Theological Seminary graduate had been a part of the Catholic Worker movement and a war tax resister for over two decades. She refers to her prison terms for civil disobedience, such as nine months in maximum security for the 1988 crime of planting corn on a nuclear missile site, as "the most significant learning experience I've had since I learned how to read." She helped organize two nonviolent "direct action" teams in

Bosnia and was one of the first internationals to visit the Palestinian refugee camp at Jenin after Israeli troops leveled it in 2002. And although she resisted having it splashed on the cover of her latest book, Kelly has been nominated three times for the Nobel peace prize.

"In 1990, when Iraq invaded Kuwait, I knew next to nothing about Iraq," she said. But following Amman Hennacy's admonition that "you can't be a vegetarian between meals, or a pacifist between wars," Kelly decided she had to do something.

> "I knew enough about world events to understand that the U.S. was not consistently opposed to one country invading another," she said. "The U.S. had only recently invaded Panama, and before that Grenada. It had supported Indonesia's invasion of East Timor. Nor was the U.S. always opposed to dictatorships. In my own neighborhood, many people arrived as refugees from brutal and ruthless dictatorships that the U.S. had supported or even installed, for example, in Chile, Guatemala, El Salvador, and Honduras. I believed that the U.S. was moving toward war with Iraq because the U.S. wanted to gain greater control over the pricing of oil and the recycling of petrodollars generated in the region. . . "

After Kelly returned to the United States, she resumed teaching, became a full time caregiver for her father, worked on disarmament campaigns, and began to forget about Iraq. "But by 1995, several of us who had been to Iraq in 1991 finally began to realize that the war had never ended. It had changed into an economic war against the weakest people in Iraq, especially children. Several of us decided to develop a campaign to end the U.S.-led UN sanctions against Iraq."

She and her fellow activists purposely violated those sanctions on a return trip to Iraq when they took medicines to Iraqi women and infants at hospitals, "which were like death rows for infants. We simply couldn't walk away from those bedsides."

So they organized Voices in the Wilderness and over the next seven years sent seventy delegations to visit Iraq and report back home what they'd learned. Delegations of about a dozen people each were composed mostly of U.S. citizens, but included Swedes, Dutch, Australians, Irish, Canadians, Scots, British, and South Koreans. Kelly's guiding hand on the tiller of this mostly volunteer effort, run out of a modest second-floor apartment on Chicago's north side, provided much of the factual and political underpinning for the antisanctions movement and eventually the peace movement trying to avert war against Iraq.

In the seven years before the 2003 U.S. invasion of Iraq, besides coordinating the logistics to send delegations, Kelly made the grueling trip to Baghdad herself twenty times, always with medical supplies in defiance of the U.S. economic embargo. She became well known in some circles in prewar Iraq, something I witnessed more than once during my first trip to Baghdad. Whether I needed office supplies, directions, or access to officials, all I needed to say was, "I'm working with Kathy Kelly," and doors were opened with a smile.

Iraqis lived with the effects of the Iran–Iraq War, which created a million casualties, the first Gulf War, then a dozen years of sanctions, and then a period of many months waiting for the skies to open up and rain cruise missiles at any moment—which they eventually did on March 20, 2003. Life under the hammer exacted a terrible toll, as Kathy described in this story she was told on a trip to Basra.

Several women in that southern Iraq city told Kathy what it was like to have imminent war hanging over their heads, day after day, for so long. "It's very hard when all you can do is sit and wait for your city to be bombed," one of them explained, describing a symptom Kathy said should be part of something called "pretraumatic stress disorder."

"They told me they had been so afraid of imminent war for so long, that when they heard a loud noise they would just inexplicably collapse," as did one Basra woman who left her house for the market one morning. Frightened by the noise of a bulldozer starting up, she passed out, fell over, hitting her head on the bulldozer, and died.

On that ride with us into Iraq in February 2003, she had no way of knowing that before she would see Chicago again she would live through three weeks of the most intense bombing in modern warfare, and greet U.S. Marines as they began the occupation of Iraq.

Less than two months after greeting those young Marines in Baghdad, Kathy was on the road in the United States, speaking about life under the bombs, captivating one audience in Detroit with stories of how individual people in Iraq dealt with seeing life as they'd known it destroyed.

- Being in Baghdad through the U.S. "shock and awe" bombing was like "going through 11 San Francisco earthquakes in one day and then getting up the next day and going through it again," she explained. The hotel where she and the Voices delegation lived, swayed back and forth from the force of the explosions. Floors shuddered. Windows were knocked out of their frames.
- The Al-Fanar Hotel staff turned the basement into a makeshift bomb shelter that grew more crowded as extended family members sought safety. With nerves frayed from a week of bombing, a Voices delegate grew impatient with how late some of the children stayed up playing games, and admonished they could "always finish the game tomorrow." An eight-year-old girl replied, "Oh no, Madame Cynthia, we might not be here tomorrow."
- One three-year-old invented a game of waving her finger in the air over and over again, calling out the word for "airplane" and then falling backwards, "dead."
- Within hours of parking their Abrams Tanks outside the hotel, the Marines blocked off streets and set up checkpoints with rolls of razor wire. "Never did I think this would happen to my country," an Iraqi woman with tears streaming down her face told Kathy. "I'm so very sad and I think this sadness will never go away."
- A doctor from Saddam City, Baghdad's poorest district, told Kelly of the surreal experience of living through bombardment and invasion after a dozen years of sanctions. "It's as though you're waking from an operation and the anesthesia starts to wear off. You still feel pain, still feel fear, but it's like having awakened from one nightmare and now you realize you're descending into another."

"But there were hopeful stories, too," Kelly told her audience: such as the architecture professor from Baghdad University who, even though the school was closed because of the war, still had his students submit their model bridge project. He also took advantage of the blacked-out skies over Baghdad to stargaze with his telescope. "You, too, must continue to enjoy the universe," he told her.

She smiled when she told the crowd in Detroit that, "the Baghdad Symphony Orchestra went ahead with their concert yesterday. That is such a particularly hopeful story," she emphasized, "because the two people who direct the orchestra had told me that they'd tried unsuccessfully to get U.S. troops to come and protect their school, the only one of its kind, designed to teach both western and eastern classical music and dance."

"The people who've been involved with it are enormously proud of what they've been able to do. For example, they have a piano with two keyboards on it, a western keyboard and an eastern keyboard. This was a place of learning, but also it was a place that was bright and fun. After being with kids on the cancer wards, with a recovery rate of 0%, I needed to be with other kids from time to time."

She recounted an earlier visit to the school. "One time I went to visit the music students after September 11 and they showed me an art exhibit they had done. One student had drawn a picture of twin towers and a jumbo jet plowing into one, which was very troubling to me, so I asked him what he was thinking about when he drew it. Was he thinking 'bull's-eye?' He answered, 'Allah wants this to happen to people in America so people in America understand what happens to people in other countries when America hit them.' Then he caught his teacher's eye and quickly added, 'and we love people in America and want to be their friend.'"

"So I started to tell them about having been in New York on September 11 and what it was like, and I realized that the people who could best understand what happened in New York and Washington were people in Iraq who had lost loved ones to war or to sanctions."

"I told the students, I'd been with people who lost their loved ones on September 11 who had carried signs from Washington to New York that said, 'Our grief is not a cry for war.' Then I told them about 150 families in New York who sang a song in the memorial service for their loved ones, an anthem that was very meaningful for people in the U.S. and Europe, which celebrated the common aspirations between people. And the kids said, 'Yes, Madame, when are you going to teach us this song?'"

"Well, Madame was in trouble because Madame's Arabic wasn't all that good. But the directors of the Baghdad Symphony, who also run the school, didn't understand the word 'can't' and within two days had transliterated the song into Arabic and taught it to the kids. The violinists knew it, the pianist knew it, and the kids were singing the song back to me."

"Before leaving Baghdad this last time," she told the Detroit crowd, "I heard that the directors of the school were not successful in getting U.S. troops to protect it from being completely ransacked in the looting that happened after Baghdad fell. I felt a remorseful twinge that I would never sing that song again. But before I came home, there was a moment of very special hope. These two directors, even though they were very depressed that so much had been lost, came to visit, carrying a gift. They gave me a tape, the only surviving tape from the school, a recording of the kids singing that song. So I'd like to sing it for you here, even though my Arabic pronunciations are terrible.

"This Is My Song" lyrics written by Lloyd Stone in the 1930s, sung to a melody by Jean Sibelius.

This Is My Song (O Finlandia)

Arabic	Transliterated	English
إلاهي لك نشيدي نشيد سلام لبلادهم وبلادي	Nesheedi Nesheed u salaam lil biladihim wa biladi	This is my home The country where my heart is Here are my dreams
هذا وطني الذي في فؤادي هنا أحلامي ومقدساتي لكن قلوب أخرى في بلاد أخرى تنبض بأحلام صادقة مثلي	Hada watani aladthi fi fuadi Huna ah lami wa mukadasati Lakin qolubun ukhra Fi biladin ukhra Tumbudhu bi ahlamin Sadikatin mithli	My hopes my holy shrine But other hearts In other lands are beating With hopes and dreams As deep and true as mine
يا إلاهي اسمع نشيدي نشيد سلام لبلادهم وبلادي	Ya ilahi isma nesheedi Nesheedu salaam Li biladihim wa biladi	Oh hear my song O God of all the nations A song of peace For their lands and for mine
	Ilahi laka	This is my song O God of all the nations A song of peace For lands afar and mine

Commenting on the U.S. invasion and occupation of Iraq, Kelly said,

The U.S. administration is hoping that the American people will agree that even though we may not find any weapons of mass destruction; even though we may not find any connection between Iraq and al Qaeda; that Saddam Hussein was indeed an evil person and it's a good thing that the U.S. got rid of him, and now we can go on to the next subject.

Many ordinary Iraqis were happy to see the Hussein government overthrown, Kelly reported. But, she added,

> The thanksgiving and jubilation were short lived, believe me. Prior to the war, half of Iraq's people were dependent on government food rations. Within a few months, nearly 100% were. The World Food Organization was ready to supply food relief for four or five months, but what after that? The wisest next steps would be to admit that we made a terrible mistake, issue timetables for withdrawal of troops, close the bases built, and work very hard to help fund reconstruction in Iraq, (with) reparations through a third party such as the United Nations.

Looking out at her audience in Detroit, Kathy's voice choked with emotion.

> We came so close to stopping this war we could almost taste it. And I can see tonight that many of you have been through the Korean war, the Vietnam war, the Guatemala war, Nicaragua, the first war in Iraq, Afghanistan, Iraq again . . . war after war after war . . . and underlying these hot wars, is a war of Western culture against the viability of Mother Earth; a war of U.S. culture against weaker countries whose resources we want to control and exploit. We went to war against Iraq because we could. The planet cannot sustain us any longer. Does all this war-making constitute an answer for future generations?

In response to her rhetorical question, Kelly believes that living a simpler life is inseparable from peacemaking, and that simpler living combined with peacemaking is the key to providing justice for people in other nations and security for people in the United States.

> If we treat other people fairly, we won't have to worry so much about living securely in this world. But in order to face the complex challenges of living in fair relationships with other people, we must grapple with the reality of our comfortable lives, in relation to tremendous need elsewhere in the world.

On the average, Americans pay over $1,500 annually "to bankroll the war machine," Kelly explained.

> But the inescapable terror that the children and grandchildren will face won't come from a handful of suicide bombers or terrorists. The inescapable terror will come from what we are doing to our planet, our air and our water. We've simply got to find a way to get an energy program for this country. And if the leaders won't put it in place then maybe we've got to find a way to ration ourselves how much energy we'll each consume, find ways to grow some of our

own food, find ways to support those networks that are in place in this country. We've got to find a different way to live and we've got to make change popular, valuable and real.

The 52-year-old activist not only sees this as her life's work but as her life's joy. She urges the thousands of people who hear her speak annually to "enjoy what we might call the further invention of nonviolence."

> We will come together to do that. As a young doctor in Iraq said to me: 'wait and see Kathy, people in your country will learn from the Iraqis.' Now I think I'm starting to get it. As we try to make these changes, we have to learn from the Iraqis, and learn from these returning Marines because they know how to live with simplicity, how to share. You know, quite a few of them said to me 'we never ever want to kill again.' Some of them even came up to us and asked, 'Will you pray for us?' Such was their remorse for what they had done in Iraq.

"My prayer for you tonight," Kelly concluded, "is that we will find ways to change; that we will be able to hear the words of Howard Zinn without rancor and maybe utter them to others: 'There is no flag large enough to cover the shame of killing innocent people.' And that one day we will come to the patriotism of Thomas Paine who said, 'My country is the world. My religion is to do good.' "

14

HOW YA GONNA KEEP 'EM DOWN ON THE INDIANA FARM (ONCE THEY'VE SEEN KERBALA?)

If Hollywood is looking for riveting dramatic material, it needs go no further than the exploits of groups like the Christian Peacemaker Teams (CPT and Voices. My nominee for a CPT scene in a movie is the story of Cliff Kindy's departure from Iraq as the U.S. invasion was in high gear.

In October 2002, with war clouds visible on the horizon, CPT sent Kindy, a 55-year-old Indiana farmer, to Baghdad to scout the possibility of bringing in a delegation, as Voices had been doing for some years. Five months and several delegations later, Kindy was still in Iraq when the skies opened up on March 20, 2003, raining cruise missiles, bunker busters, daisy cutters, cluster bombs, napalm, and every other explosive device in the Pentagon's inventory short of nuclear weapons.

Within two weeks, U.S. Marines were at the approaches to Baghdad. Kindy, about two dozen CPT delegates, and some fifteen Voices delegates were hunkered down in three small hotels, directly across the Tigris River from the most heavily bombed Iraqi government buildings, including some of Saddam Hussein's palaces.

"The Mukhabarat (Iraqi secret police) was getting more uptight as U.S. troops got closer to Baghdad," Cliff recalled. "One morning a missile hit closer than ever to our hotel, taking out a communications center and we lost our land phones completely. A couple of us went to the phone center to see what happened. The owner of a restaurant right across the street saw us and invited us to inspect the damage to his place also from the missile strike. We crossed the street to look and took some pictures of his restaurant."

With U.S. soldiers on the outskirts of Baghdad, American civilians, even Church of the Brethren farmers with long, grey beards like Kindy's, set off Mukhabarat alarm bells by taking photographs near a bombed communications center. Cliff and his friends were quickly apprehended, driven across town, and told to leave the country immediately.

The CPT detainees argued with their Iraqi "minder," whom they suspected had high security connections, that making the twelve-hour drive across the desert at night during the height of the bombing was, at the least, unsafe and possibly deadly. The authorities relented and told them they would have to leave the next morning.

At 9:30 A.M. on March 29, three taxis with the deported CPTers and a few others who decided to leave headed for Amman, Jordan.

About three-fourths of the way to the Jordanian border, the third taxi with Cliff and four others in it hit a piece of shrapnel at over 90 mph, blew a tire, and went off the road into a shallow ditch. All five were injured, some with broken bones. Kindy received a nasty gash in his head. The drivers of the other two taxis apparently did not notice they'd lost the last vehicle and kept going.

The next driver traveling that route noticed the crashed taxi and stopped to help, driving the injured to the nearest place with a medical facility, the village of Rutbah.

> "We were taken to a makeshift clinic," Kindy recalled. "The first-aid people we initially saw greeted us and said 'it doesn't matter if you are Iraqi, Muslim, or whatever, we will treat your injuries.' Then I learned from the doctor, as he put ten stitches in my head without any anesthetic, that Rutbah's small hospital, an electrical station, and a communications center had been bombed by a U.S. warplane just three days before. I thought, 'Wow, here we are from the same country as the bomber and yet he's saving our lives.' "

On the highway, a car of Somali students who had earlier rescued the three-vehicle caravan from running out of gas appeared again. The young people recognized Cliff's taxi lying off the road, so they stopped to help once more. Finding the taxi deserted, they correctly assumed the passengers had made their way to Rutbah, and so hurried to catch the remaining two taxis. Near the Jordanian border, the students caught up with them and helped the passengers convince the drivers to go back into the danger zone to pick up Cliff and his colleagues waiting in Rutbah.

Once everyone assembled at the border crossing, it happened that the Somalis came to the rescue yet again. One of the injured travelers, a Mennonite minister from Seattle whose ribs had been broken in the crash, blacked out in the visa room. Iraqi immigration officials, still in charge of the crossing for a few more days, asked for assistance. One of the Somalis, a medical student, stepped forward to help.

The piece of shrapnel lying on the road that began this chain of events was fateful in another way as well. There had been scattered reports coming from international reporters in Iraq that U.S. warplanes and cruise missiles had bombed hospitals and civilian infrastructure in the opening days of "shock and awe." Pentagon officials denied the reports. However, the eyewitness accounts provided by the CPT members and a Japanese journalist traveling with them disproved the Pentagon's denials. When the contingent finally reached Amman, their story and photographs of Rutbah were in big demand.

Kindy has told this story many times, always in the same matter-of-fact way. Not until pressed for more details did he acknowledge just how frightening the whole ordeal was.

> Looking back on what happened, I think the medical people in Rutbah didn't believe I was going to make it, since I was the last person they treated. While I waited for them, I remember standing outside myself and looking at Cliff Kindy lying on the bed. I knew that I had been like this before . . . that this wasn't hard to deal with . . . that I'd had a lot of bonuses and had been gifted with life beyond what I thought I would have, like the time in Gaza in 1993 when Israeli soldiers raided the Palestinian home I was staying in. I watched Cliff to see what he was going to decide—was he going to stay there awake, or was he going to close his eyes and die?

♦ ♦ ♦

Less than a year after Cliff's dramatic exit, I found myself back in what was now occupied Baghdad, enjoying breakfast tea with him at the CPT apartment along the Tigris River.

"Do you think you could help us get some press on this new report we've just finished?" Cliff asked. Glad to renew my friendship with this affable Hoosier whom I had met just before the U.S. invasion, I wanted to be helpful. But the thing uppermost on my mind that morning was the plague of mosquito bites I'd gotten after a night as a CPT guest.

It was January and cold, but apparently not cold enough in central Baghdad to eradicate the tiny menaces. I scratched and complained ungraciously, comforting myself with the fact that the permanent lodgings I'd find later that day would be several blocks farther from the river.

The mosquitoes should have reminded me not to sweat the small stuff in the face of momentous developments. The document Cliff was talking about, "Report and Recommendations on Iraqi Detainees", had just been released days earlier. Delivered to the ruling Coalition Provisional Authority and urging "immediate attention," it condemned what it concluded was a pattern of violent house raids, conducted by the U.S. military, resulting in the roundups of thousands of Iraqis and the theft of their private property. It highlighted the stories of seventy-two individuals detained and thrown into Saddam Hussein's prison system now run by the Americans. One facility just west of Baghdad was Abu Ghraib.

The report alleged serious violations of the Geneva Conventions, and some of the stories were hard to believe. Having arrived less than twenty-four hours earlier, I was just beginning to make my way through the looking glass into occupied Iraq. Listening to the gray-bearded farmer stoically relate abuse after abuse, I did not want to believe these could be anything but isolated incidents. Nevertheless, by the end of our meeting I could not avoid asking myself, "Could America have adopted such inhumane and disastrously stupid policies at the very outset of the occupation?" Four months later, when the world read the stories and, more importantly, saw the pictures of dead and tortured prisoners at Abu Ghraib, the answer to that question was clear.

For the first time, I passed up the opportunity to be a movement P.R. agent and stuck to the reason that brought me back to Iraq: to work as a journalist.

I decided the best I could do with my limited time and money in Iraq was to follow up two or three of the cases in the CPT report. Doing so required spending weeks with the peacemaker team, the families of detainees, and the military.

The cases I decided to follow happened to be in two hot spots of what was becoming known as "the Sunni Triangle," the farming villages of Abu Siffa and Abu Hishma, both about forty miles north of Baghdad near the town of Balad, and a village called al-Jazeera, sixty miles west of the capital city, beyond Fallujah and just outside Ramadi. On long, dusty trips in a lurching van, I met other CPT members and learned of lifetimes devoted to peacemaking in conflict zones around the globe.

Influenced by Gandhi and Martin Luther King Jr., the organization officially describes itself as "an independent, faith-based, violence-reduction

CPT member Jim Loney at a vigil for Iraqi detainees in a busy Baghdad square, February, 2004. (*Photo by Mike Ferner*)

project supported by Christian churches across North America." Unofficially, they like to say they stand on the side of those who have the guns pointed at them. The group's slogan is "Getting in the Way," a double reference to obstructing violence or following Christ's way.

As the U.S. occupation of Iraq deepened, the CPT mission expanded to include helping Iraqis find family members detained by the U.S. military and lost in the prison system now administered by the Americans, conducting public vigils on behalf of the detainees, and talking with Muslim clerics interested in replicating the peace team's methods among their own faithful.

Kindy's most recent trip began right after the 2004 U.S. presidential elections, just as the Bush administration began its second siege of Fallujah. "Right after the hospitals were bombed," he added, which opened the attack on the city of 300,000.

> We wanted to get into Fallujah, but we just couldn't for quite a while. So we met with refugees from there in several different locations until just last month (March 2005) when we finally got in. We were working with a local human rights committee and they told us there was a ninety-nine percent chance we couldn't get past the U.S. checkpoints around Fallujah. Well, a one percent chance sounds pretty good to CPTers, so we gave it a try. Our group was in the second and third of three cars, with women and medical supplies in the first. Soldiers searched them thoroughly so we simply told them 'we're with the first car,' and they let us right through.

In an interview in April 2005, a month after returning from his third five-month trip, Kindy said,

> This last trip has been more difficult. I began to realize that it *has* affected me to be in a war zone. After the first two trips I thought 'I can handle this,' but not after this one. We were all under more stress as a result of the tighter security. We didn't get out as much; couldn't walk or travel freely like we had before. In the past, I had heard people talk about PTSD (Posttraumatic Stress Disorder), but now I realize that I'm impacted by it, too.

Cliff began dreaming about the thieves who got into their apartment in central Baghdad, tied them up, and threatened to kill them before stealing computers that had irreplaceable photographs and data. "I started to imagine what it would be like to get your head cut off, or I'd get terrified and my imagination would run wild at the sound of a key going into a door . . . " his voice trailed off. "We started taking extra precautions. We quit taking taxis and only used our hired drivers and vans; we varied pickup times and places; had our worship upstairs so people walking by wouldn't hear English – lots of little things."

As violence exploded following the devastation of Fallujah, Cliff said their Iraqi friends and other NGOs counseled them to leave, but except for a break of a couple of weeks, they didn't. During this period, even organizations with decades of experience in war zones like CARE had pulled their staff out of Baghdad because of escalating violence. "We felt alone, being the only western NGO in Baghdad and the so-called Sunni Triangle area."

"One way I noticed it was affecting us," he explained, "was after we'd been there about two months. I could tell members of the team were getting more irritable; we didn't have the patience we usually had."

He said he experienced times when his spirit was "too mixed up – too disoriented to hear God's nudges," which he described as getting a feel for when to step back and be patient, or go ahead and take a risk.

> One of the things about living with more security measures is that it closes your operating space—out of fear, I guess. It closes off opportunities to invite others to withdraw from the violence they may be involved in, whether it's a guerilla fighter in Colombia or a paramilitary on the Magdalena River, or when deciding to go into a U.S. military base, or to meet with (Muqtadah al) Sadr's representatives. It reduces the chances for reconciliations. It also makes me recognize my own complicity in violence.
>
> Each time I return from a trip like this I find it's very healing to get back to the garden. This year I guess I need more healing. I find myself asking 'maybe I should take a leave..how long do people do this kind of work . . . do we build up calluses and start to lose the compassion that is so important . . . will I get that way . . . How are we changed by this work?' This year I feel like I'm beginning to get some answers.

The organic farmer and activist said that one of the things that made his last trip worthwhile was when several clerics asked for assistance to start up a Muslim Peacemaker Team modeled on CPT.

This embryonic effort had its beginnings in Kerbala, where Shi'ite imams expressed interest in the idea, and was later picked up by a sheik at Abu Hanife, the largest Sunni mosque in Baghdad. After the CPT conducted a five-day training with the group in Kerbala, Kindy reported that "they're now talking about doing their own training which we think is a great idea. They won't have to go through translators. They'll be able to own the process if they do it themselves."

And in the latest development, Kindy said CPT members in Baghdad were contacted by a Christian priest who expressed interest in broadening participation beyond Muslims, to more of an interfaith, Iraq Peacemaker Team. "So far, the group in Kerbala is still a Muslim Peacemaker Team, but who know what kinds of other peacemaker teams might spring up, not just religious ones. The possibilities are exciting!"

Some of the initial ideas mentioned for peacemaker team projects, Kindy reported, were helping with cleanup in Fallujah, sending a team to Darfur, and sending peacemaker training teams to places around Iraq.

◆ ◆ ◆

This work has brought CPT into close working relationships with Sunni and Shiite imams, tribal sheiks, farmers, Army officers, and human rights attorneys. One incident illustrates how wide the circle was in which they worked.

One particularly dusty February day, I was bouncing in the back of the van CPT had hired for a two-day visit to Abu Hishma. En route, I learned this was the village the Army had surrounded with razor wire as a response to a fatal Iraqi attack on an armored personnel carrier on patrol. Cliff said it would be a good idea to meet the Lieutenant Colonel in charge of the battalion, Nathan Sassaman, and inquire about spending some time with his unit.

Hours later, we arrived at Forward Operations Base, Paliwoda, named after one of Sassaman's captains killed in an Iraqi mortar attack. We greeted the sunburned young soldiers guarding the gate, who told us their commanding officer had just left for a meeting in Balad and we might catch him on the way out. Moments later, two Humvees and two Bradley Fighting Vehicles roared through the gate in thick billows of dust.

Cliff waved expectantly and the vehicles ground to a halt. Sassaman emerged from one of the Bradleys to meet Cliff, leaving a Sergeant at-ease in the turret behind a fifty-caliber machine gun.

The organic farmer from Indiana and the former quarterback of the 1984 Army football team shook hands and caught up on the small talk of the day. Only partially joking, Cliff invited Sassaman to join CPT upon his retirement.

Standing outside Forward Operations Base Paliwoda, near the town of Balad, 1st Battalion Commander, Lt. Col. Nathan Sassaman talks with three local tribal leaders, or sheiks. (*Photo by Mike Ferner*).

The Lieutenant Colonel put Cliff off with a smile, saying he would first have to "ask Mrs. Sassaman how she felt about that."

After Cliff introduced us, Sassaman skirted days of red tape and invited me with a casual "what're you doing next Tuesday?" We confirmed my visit and before turning to leave, three local sheiks walked up, greeted Sassaman and engaged him in conversation. I observed the four men talking in the bright afternoon sun, knowing there was everylikelihood they would exchange mortar fire later that night.

If Cliff Kindy lives to have grandchildren, he will have stories to tell them far beyond the drought of '88 or those blue-ribbon strawberries at the county fair.

15

FROM AN ACT OF DESPERATION TO A MILLION HITS A DAY

"I didn't really plan to be a journalist. It was more an act of desperation . . . desperation I felt as I watched the war coming closer."

That's how the most influential independent journalist covering the occupation of Iraq described his entry into the dicey trade of twenty-first century war correspondents. His actual entry into Iraq, however, was anything but auspicious.

Through mid-2002, war drums emanating from Washington, D.C grew louder, foreshadowing the March 2003 U.S. invasion of Iraq. Dahr Jamail, a mountain-climbing guide in his mid-thirties from Anchorage, Alaska, felt he had to do something significant in response. He had been emailing a couple Internet writers to get tips for a trip to Lebanon to visit his cousins. But, growing more discontented with the mainstream news media's coverage of the lead-up to war, he decided to ask his contacts if they could instead advise him how to get to Baghdad so he could observe and write.

I met Dahr at the Agadir Hotel in central Baghdad, the cheapest lodgings I could find in a hurry when I returned there in January 2004. Just ten days away from finishing his first visit, he had already begun to make his mark as an independent journalist and would return three more times. The next opportunity we had to sit and talk at length was in August 2005, at the Veterans For Peace convention in Dallas, where he was scheduled to be one of the main speakers.

The afternoon before his talk, I asked him to describe how and why a mountain-climbing guide from Alaska became an independent journalist in Iraq.

Dahr Jamail (DJ): When I asked the guys I'd been emailing about the Lebanon trip if they could tell me how to get into Iraq instead, they were like, "yeah, you can do it . . . this is how . . . go to this hotel in Jordan . . . get a car there . . . this is how much you should pay 'em . . . ,' they basically gave me like this individual 'Lonely Planet' guide on how to get into Baghdad. Both of them told me to go to the Fanar Hotel, but the day before I went in was when the donkey cart blasted the Palestine Hotel . . . and I started shittin' kittens! (Iraqi resistance fighters scored direct hits on the Palestine, across the street from the al-Fanar, with a rocket launcher mounted on a donkey cart.) So I emailed these guys and they said, 'naw, don't worry, it's OK, it's OK . . . but maybe (the Fanar) is not so safe, so go to the Agadir.'

M Ferner (MF): What made you want to go to Iraq to write in the first place?

DJ: Becoming a journalist was really an act of desperation. I saw the lead-up to the invasion and I was reading everything I could get my hands on. I could tell it was bullshit. I could tell it was lies. It was about oil and strategic positioning. So I did the usual things we do to express dissent. You know. I went to demonstrations; I tried to educate people; I tried to educate myself more; I wrote letters to my senators; made phone calls; signed petitions; all the stuff we're supposed to do.

And then I saw February 15, '03 come and go. (On that day, millions of people around the world protested the likely U.S. invasion of Iraq.) Nothing changed, and then the invasion. I was horrified. I would sit up at nights and listen to *BBC Radio* or read the Internet to watch what was happening in Iraq. And I was just . . . I was losing it.

At the same time, when I saw or heard Bush talk I was on the brink of having an aneurism. And I just decided, 'I've gotta do something else. I've gotta take it to the next level. I've got to do *something* to at least put my drop in the bucket.'

I'm not married, I don't have kids, and I started saving money because I got this idea that maybe I could go over there and just report, because I felt that these bastards were getting away with it because of the media—that if the American people had half an idea what was really going on, they wouldn't stand for it. And so I figured what my two cents would be; well, I'll just go over there and try to report it myself.

MF: Had you done any journalism before that?

DJ: I'd done a little freelancing for a weekly alternative paper we've got in Anchorage. I was writing mountain-climbing stories and we started getting political after 9/11 and after about a month of that we were doing some good articles—like 'why did this happen? Well, let's look at our policy in Afghanistan and let's look at what Reagan did.' Well, they fired the editor, and that really put the lid back on my pressure cooker because then I had nowhere to write. Then everything led up to the invasion and something had to give.

MF: Once you were in Baghdad, how did you get around, get a translator, and so forth?

DJ: Just to show you how serendipitous the whole thing's been, I delayed my trip (from Amman, Jordan to Baghdad, in November 2003) for a couple days because of the donkey cart attack. I was at the hotel (in Amman) and

James Longley, the filmmaker, had just come out of Iraq. He'd spent a ton of time there, before, during and after the invasion. We started talking and he told me how to get a hold of his interpreter in Baghdad. Stuff like that just kept working out.

I started out sending emails to 130 people—just dispatches to 130 people that wanted to know what was goin' on. Then after a few weeks, I ran into someone who told me 'you should post on *Electronic Iraq*,' so I started doing that and that was really the launching pad. *Flashpoints* and *BBC Radio* started interviewing me and, at the end of that trip, the *New Standard* (an electronic newspaper) found me and I began to get paid for some of my work.

MF: That was near the time your first trip ended, and then what?

DJ: Then I came back to the states and started giving presentations and raising some money. The *New Standard* helped organize a speaking tour and things were really, really tight, but I soon had enough money to go back for another few months, beginning in April '04.

I could tell on that second trip that my stuff was starting to get out . . . going into Fallujah and writing about that and the torture . . . there was so much kicking off and people really started to respond to my writing. I decided that although it was fine working for The *New Standard*, I might as well be fully independent.

On the second trip, I wrote for *New Standard, Interpress,* and *Islam Online*. Those gigs plus some online fundraising covered my costs and allowed me to save for another trip.

When I went back home for several months after that second trip, I was busy doing lots of presentations and radio interviews, funding myself by passing the hat after personal appearances. One of my first presentations was in Berkeley, California, where a friend of one of my mountain-climbing buddies lived. He created a website I could use for posting reports from my third trip that started in November 2004.

That third trip was a turning point. I knew they (U.S. military forces) were about to siege Fallujah right after the U.S. elections. I flew out of JFK the evening of November 2, 2004, the day of the elections. When I left, Kerry was just barely behind. When I landed in Amman, I was talking with this woman on the plane and she'd called her dad back in the states, and I could tell by the look on her face that he (Bush) had won. It was just really an intense time to be going over there. About two days later, I was flying into Baghdad and just a few days after that they started the siege of Fallujah.

As far as I know, I was the only non-embedded American journalist there and I was just working my ass off, writing for *Interpress,* on *Flashpoints,* and then on *Democracy Now,* which really brought it to a whole other level as far as how many people were listening to and reading my stuff.

A lot of times we think that 'well, we're just alternative media and people aren't really following us,' but I'd like to point out that for whatever the reasons, there were times from early November to mid-December, 2004, when my site was getting a million hits a day. We had to upgrade the server three times in one week. It was just goin' off the charts. That just showed me that people are just desperate for the truth . . . desperate for real news. The people know that the jig is up on mainstream media and they respond. When you put your ass on the line and go out there to get 'em that information, they respond and they'll support it. People were donating to the site. I was getting so many amazing emails from people . . . it was really incredible.

MF: Then you took another break?

DJ: Yeah, came out to Jordan for a break and went to Egypt to do some scuba diving in the Red Sea, then went back in early January for a month to stay for the quote-unquote elections.

That was another really intense trip. There was an incredible amount of violence. It was super tense. The election was just a debacle, such a sham. Reporting on that was a full time job. There were days on that trip when I was getting twelve or thirteen radio calls a day and writing for several publications. I had more work than I could do, sometimes writing two stories a day. It was a ridiculous pace. That's how I dealt with my nerves . . . I was a workaholic. I got up and turned on my computer while I was going to brush my teeth.

I wrote early in the morning, and then my translator came by, we'd go out to cover a story, and I'd write it up later in the day.

In February 2005, I came back home . . . did *lots* of presentations. In fact, if all I wanted to do was presentations, I could do that for six months straight right now. I hired a friend to be my presentations coordinator . . . it's just really exploded beyond belief and I've just been goin with it. It just feels like 'hey, I'm makin' a difference and it feels really good . . . the bigger the platform I get, the louder I want to talk and I'm just gonna keep doin' it. I have this signature on my Yahoo email, an Orwell quote that says 'During times of universal deceit, telling the truth becomes a revolutionary act,' and that's what it feels like. We're like half a step away from fascist lockdown in my opinion, and the time to speak out is now. So now I've got a voice to use, to give other people a voice who don't have one, like the IVAW (Iraq Veterans Against the War) guys, and people at this convention . . . I just feel I've been given this job to do and I can do it, and I'm gonna keep doin' it."

MF: Are you planning on going back?

DJ: I definitely want to go back to Iraq although I don't really know when . . . I'm looking at writing a book, doing more presentations, more conferences . . . but it's great. It's been one hell of a ride and I wouldn't trade one second of it.

16

HANGING WITH THE 1st BATTALION, 4th INFANTRY DIVISION

FORWARD OPERATIONS BASE (FOB) PALIWODA

I arrived at this dusty dot on the map one day in late February to eat, sleep, and patrol for a couple days with the soldiers of the Army's 1st Battalion, 4th Infantry Division who call FOB Paliwoda "home."

Near the town of Balad, forty-some miles north of Baghdad, the base occupies a former Iraqi school. It is named after Eric Paliwoda, a 28 year-old Army captain from Goodyear, Arizona, killed by an Iraqi mortar six weeks earlier.

The first guard station inside the perimeter fence is staffed by two young GIs, including a redhead from New Jersey, working on a sunburn in what is still officially winter. He announced to the battalion office that Lorna Tychostup, editor for *Chronogram Magazine,* and I had arrived. As he hung up the phone, mortars landed with muffled explosions in the distance.

Arriving at the battalion headquarters we were met by Captain Blake, an administrative law officer, who extended a welcoming hand and seemed glad for the conversation while we waited at the office for his commanding officer, Lieutenant Colonel Nathan Sassaman.

The youthful-looking captain told us about his duties at the local municipality, where once a week he listened to claims from Iraqi civilians and decided who would be awarded compensation. "I've heard thousands of cases . . . every story you can imagine," Blake said. "I try to award compensation when I can . . . when they've got some kind of proof of what happened. For example, if an Iraqi tells me that his car was damaged on the highway by a tire falling off one of our trucks, and he's got the tire to prove it, well, I'll compensate him."

Blake stopped another captain hurrying by so he could introduce us. Well over six feet, with close-cropped blond hair, the base military intelligence officer was a walking bundle of energy. He asked how I got to the base and when I responded "by taxi," he blew up and fairly shouted, "You trying to get yourself killed?" He added that the only way to travel on highways outside of Baghdad was in an armored SUV, preferably with an armed escort.

There was no point in arguing with someone who never left the base in anything lighter than an armored personnel carrier (APC), but I couldn't disagree more with his reasoning. For over a month, I had felt perfectly safe traveling in Baghdad and throughout the "Sunni Triangle" in nondescript beat-up taxis that didn't attract the attention of thieves or resistance fighters. Our military hosts and high-rolling contractors acted on a shared belief: security is achieved with armor, armed guards, and horsepower. To independent journalists, however, safety is gained by swimming with the local fish, not identifying yourself as rich, foreign, or military. To be sure, it was the only transportation we could afford, but besides being safer, it offered stories we'd never see or hear from inside the tinted glass of what I jokingly referred to as an SMV—a "Shoot Me Vehicle."

A few minutes later, Colonel Sassaman returned from a meeting in the nearby village of Abu Hishma. He said hello and extended an invitation to go out on patrol.

Helmeted, flak-jacketed, and sitting in the back seat of a humvee, I went with two GIs as we rolled out of FOB Paliwoda in late afternoon. Accompanying us on the patrol were two other humvees, a Bradley Fighting Vehicle, and a constant cloud of fine, gray dust.

Adam Tymensky, a young staff sergeant from Novi, Michigan, turned to show me on the map where we'd be going: sectors A, B, and C, outside the town of Balad. His battalion was due to leave Iraq in about a month. The driver, another youthful GI, Sergeant Brad Contat, said he was from Maumee, Ohio. We noted that the three of us lived within an hour's drive from each other, back home.

I asked about the infamously hot Iraq summers and if the pace slows to compensate for it. "Oh, no," Tymensky replies. "We keep doing patrols. Just pound down more water."

"What's the hottest you saw here last summer?"

"The hottest we recorded was 142 degrees . . . in the shade. It was 150 in the sun. That was the day the colonel's watch blew up . . . just fell apart on him," the Sergeant said with a chuckle.

He explained that we'd make a routine check of sites from which Iraqis have launched mortars against the base. "They use 60s (60 mm), 81s, and 120s against us. They can use our 82-mm tubes for their 81s, but we can't use their 81s with our 82s. We use radar to track where they come from," the sergeant responded to my question. "That, plus we measure the impact holes to figure the size of the mortar they used and the direction it was fired from."

We drove down dirt roads and farm lanes just like the ones I visited with the CPT on earlier visits to Abu Hishma, when we listened to villagers' accounts of midnight house raids and how their relatives were apprehended by Colonel Sassaman's battalion. A grove of blooming apricot trees gave an air of bucolic peacefulness, abruptly ended when we "dismounted" and quietly walked the rest of the lane single-file.

After a short walk, we found a small depression of freshly disturbed earth nestled among the oranges and apricots, signifying where Iraqis had placed a mortar tube. Contat noted "We check on 'em just to let 'em know *we* know where they are." Tymensky added, "Sometimes we'll drop a 2,000 pound bomb on a mortar site. We'll call in the Air Force F-16s . . . we've done three of them."

The light faded as we returned to the humvees. The patrol drove to a wide spot in the dirt road and set up a temporary checkpoint. As two of the soldiers chatted about what movie would be playing back at the base, three others stood in the road, ready to signal drivers to stop. In the space of twenty minutes, four small pickup trucks were pulled over, the cabs searched, and the vehicles waved on their way.

Sassaman explained that he keeps the patrols rolling on a regular basis "so we can see what's going on. If something happens, we'll be out here already, able to respond quicker."

By the time we resumed the patrol, the sun had set. Forty miles beyond the lights of Baghdad, outside the small town of Balad, night fell heavily and it was almost moonless as well. "Seventeen percent illumination tonight," Tymensky confirmed.

The patrol drove single file in the dark, with no headlights. Two tiny taillights glowed dimly on the back of a Bradley in front of us, invisible except at very close range. In between the clouds of dust, it was actually easier to see the Bradley when it got a little farther away and became a barely perceptible silhouette against an eighty-three percent black sky. Despite night vision goggles, the soldiers said that it was still tough to see with that little illumination.

I barely made out that we were driving atop an irrigation canal dike. The "road" was narrow, no wider than a single traffic lane at its widest. Ten feet below us, down a steep bank, the canal water flowed slowly. Suddenly, the number of drowning deaths I'd read among the casualty lists began to make sense.

Back at the base, it was time to try MREs (Meals Ready to Eat). Iraqi workers under contract with Haliburton Corporation, with an armed U.S. military escort, delivered one hot meal per day in the afternoon. The rest of the time soldiers chose from a handful of MREs, including grilled chicken breast. Seeing a messmate open a hermetically sealed packet containing a piece of preserved, cooked, white meat, and wondering how many years it had waited to see the light of day prompted me to choose the black bean and cheese enchilada.

"But you gotta microwave it, man!"

"No you don't! To get the whole MRE experience it's gotta be uncooked. But you gotta . . . oh jeez; he's eating it without the picante!"

Having survived an uncooked enchilada without picante sauce and a version of Seven-up, it was time for nightly ablutions and bed. Wakeup call for the next patrol would come soon, at 3:30 A.M.

Outside at the latrine, I struck up a conversation with Sergeant Collado who was catching a smoke. In what seemed like a rather bizarre accommodation to the times, the barracks is a no-smoking zone—meaning that at any minute you could get "lit up" by an Iraqi mortar falling on your head while you're inside the barracks, but you couldn't "light up" for health reasons.

Collado informed me that eating too many MREs would make your urine smell like preservatives, so he stayed away from them whenever possible. How many MREs that would take and what preservative-laced urine smelled like were questions I was glad not to be around long enough to answer.

The sergeant was on his second, three-year enlistment. His response to the standard "How are you doing?" brought a sad-sounding reply that he was getting a divorce. "A third of everybody's marriage on this tour of duty ends that way. It's a casualty you don't see." He quickly changed the subject, explaining he was a mortarman and to "not be rattled in a little while when we send over some 120s (120-mm mortars, only 5 mm smaller than the gun on an Abrams tank) at 9 o'clock."

The night was windy and the temperature was supposed to reach the mid-twenties. Even though Captain Blake made sure I had a blanket and a small portable heater in the small room, fixing the window blown out by a recent mortar attack became a priority. A helpful medic rounded up some plastic and tape and a minute before 9:00 P.M., I finished patching the window. At exactly the top of the hour, the first of a dozen loud "whumps" resounded, snapping the plastic windowpane taut each time.

Even with the window fixed, the light jacket I brought with me from Baghdad and one blanket was not nearly enough to keep warm. A fitful few hours passed and a knock on the door said it was time for the next patrol.

The night was quiet, cold, and clear. Tychostup and I walked out to where two Bradleys idled. An APC appeared in a minute and we were invited aboard with a captain and two sergeants. We left FOB Paliwoda to patrol the area around Abu Hishma for the next eight hours. Very quickly, I learned that our APC had been pressed into service from the repair shop where it was waiting to get the heater fixed. A little later, I learned that our visit meant the two sergeants had been given an extra night's duty to accompany us, but they never once complained about it.

The top hatch stayed open during the patrol and the wind whipping in was below freezing. I made sure my jacket was zipped, turned up the collar, and took a seat on a shaky box of bottled water on the floor. Two boxes near my feet look sturdier, but I kept the seat I had. One of the boxes was marked "Dynamite," and the other said "C-4 Explosive." Without detonators, they were safe. But if they did go, we would all be dead instantly so it didn't matter where any of us sat—there was just something about the idea of actually putting my ass on a box of high explosives that I didn't like.

When we were barely outside the gate, it became clear we wouldn't have any conversations while on patrol. It was impossible to hear anything except a noise best described as 100 hammers hitting the outside of a steel drum as hard as possible . . . while you're inside it. The APC, like the Bradley, is a tracked vehicle and as the tracks go round, they make a hellish noise.

A factory-installed sign across from my perch read: "HEARING DANGER! DOUBLE EAR PROTECTION REQUIRED!" Upfront, the driver wore a pair of ear muff-style protectors, but neither the captain nor the sergeants had any. Not wanting to look like a wimp, I only put my fingers in my ears part of the time, but the roar was literally deafening. I couldn't help but think those guys were losing some of their hearing every time they went on patrol in these vehicles.

They rolled down the dirt roads around Abu Hishma. A thick cloud of the fine grayish tan powder swirled about us constantly, blew into the open hatch, coating us inside and out. By dawn, my face was caked and stiff. If the dust had been black, we would've all looked like coal miners at the end of a shift.

If you ask most soldiers about their duty in Iraq they tell you they're "doing a job." It's dangerous and unusual, but in a way that's what it is—a job. Thinking back to some of the more beastly jobs I've had, I realized that these soldiers were workers in uniforms. Even if they never got shot at once during their whole tour of duty, they were getting used up. They were losing their hearing, filling their lungs with grit, depleted uranium dust, and who knows what else. They were being ground up in the service of empire, occupying a nation that didn't want them.

We stopped for a break and when my ears quit ringing enough to hear, I asked the three GIs, "Why do *you* think you're here?"

The young captain from Michigan, not long out of West Point, answered, "To get rid of Saddam Hussein; to give the Iraqis their freedom; to fight terrorism." A bone-tired sergeant from West Virginia looked me straight in the eye and said, "You know, I don't really know *why* I'm here." His comrade, just as tired, from North Dakota, replied with a single word: "Oil."

I asked them what they thought of Iraq. The sergeant from West Virginia, whose wife was getting a degree in social work back home, said, "You start to see some little results. If you came back in a year, you'd probably see more. People here have something they've never had before—a chance. It's something we gave them and what they do with it is up to them."

"Would you ever want to come back as a tourist?"

"No. I don't care if I ever see this place again. I've made a lot of good friends with the guys and all, but I wouldn't want to come back here."

He thought for a second and added, "Maybe in 50 years they'll make something of this place. People here are very ingenuitive [*sic*] . . . they can make something out of damn near nothin.' With a little education I'm sure they could make a go of it."

The sun came finally up in a cloudless sky and was a welcome sight. We had stopped on a hilltop with a commanding view of Abu Hishma and environs.

As my legs began to thaw and bend, I walked over to one of the Bradleys. The first person I saw was a woman GI who introduced herself as the patrol's medic. I tried to engage her in conversation about having done the same job in the Navy years ago. Her "so what?" look of response made me feel like a very old duffer and I left it at that.

We left the hilltop and approached Abu Hishma in the daylight. We stopped at the gate constructed in the ring of razor wire this battalion threw up around the village three months earlier—the day 26-year-old Sergeant Dale Panchot was killed by an armor-piercing, rocket-propelled grenade that I was told sliced through the Bradley he rode in and lodged in his chest. Several adults and children were already standing around at that early hour as we passed through the gate. I stood in the APC, my head and shoulders visible through the open hatch. The view was very different from what I saw walking these same lanes with the CPT.

Even though I wore a flak jacket and pushed my helmet down as far as possible on my head, one of the kids pointed to me. Rubbing his chin to indicate a beard like mine, he hollered to one of his buddies. My heart sank and I wished we could stop so I could explain that I'm a journalist, and this is what journalists do. It shouldn't have, but it felt like a betrayal of their trust.

I didn't ask my companions in the APC, but the question came to mind: How can you literally look down on the Iraqi people from an armored vehicle and not feel somehow in command? Or how can you be an Iraqi looking up at the Bradleys and APCs, hear the roaring engines, and not feel occupied?

We traversed the roads and lanes of Abu Hishma, dragging along our mini dust storm. When it broke enough to see people standing below us, the captain smiled and waved at every kid along the way. He said this was the favorite part of his day. Nearly all of the kids and about half of the adults returned his greeting. Those who didn't, gazed back with a much more somber look than the youngsters' smiles.

As we turned a sharp ninety-degree corner, we passed a family's laundry put out to dry on the front-yard fence. Did they routinely rewash it after a patrol passed, or did they just accept that their laundry was never going to be clean as long as the American patrols went by? I ate and breathed Abu Hishma for one eight-hour patrol. The soldiers did every other day for their year tour of duty. The people who call Abu Hishma home endured it every single day for as long as the occupation lasts.

Off to the right was an apple orchard or an orange grove. It was hard to tell. The tree trunks were blackened, leaves gone, grass burned. With the excitement of a kid playing with a new laboratory kit, one of the sergeants pointed out the sight and explained what happened.

> We were getting mortared from around here, so a couple weeks ago we came by to send them a message. We spread out a bunch of (55-gallon) barrels of homemade napalm (Styrofoam dissolved in gasoline), put some C-4 on each one, wired 'em together and blew 'em up. You shoulda seen it! It didn't do as good a job as it should've though. I guess we didn't make the napalm thick enough.

About 11:00 A.M., the patrol ended and we headed back to the base. After sitting exhausted in a sunny spot for a few minutes, I thanked my lucky stars that my visit with the 4th Infantry Division was at an established base—with portable shower units—instead of rolling hell-bent through Iraq like they were six months earlier.

Soon it was time for lunch and the day's hot meal was unloaded from a truck by Iraqis. Going through the chow line we were served a good, tasty meal: grilled, marinated chicken strips, flavorful pinto beans, salad, desert, coffee, milk, and soft drinks. Oddly enough, the most exotic-looking dish was the salad, made of generic iceberg lettuce. The pale green salad staple, common in the United States, is rarely seen in Iraq. The local variety, a deep green romaine, is a common vector for intestinal diseases and studiously avoided by Westerners who've not yet developed resistance to the region's water-borne illnesses.

The XO of the battalion, Major Rob Gwinner, visited after lunch and readily agreed to an interview in the warm sunshine.

He listed the various Army units, including his, that were scheduled to be replaced in a couple of weeks and described how the shift would be made. "Countless hours will be spent in the transition, going over trends we've observed that dictate how to fight and respond. The guys coming in are fresh. They've been in Kosovo. As long as they execute as we tell them, any group of the enemy who goes toe to toe with them will lose every time."

"The enemy has changed tactics" in the second half of his battalion's year-long tour of duty, Gwinner explained. "Before that, they operated with cells of maybe fifteen guys. We've destroyed several of them and another one pops up. These are guys who probably never liked Americans anyway, who're paid a couple thousand dollars to shoot RPGs at us. But we killed or captured many of them."

Then, the XO continued, the Iraqis started using simple IEDs , followed by larger, more complex ones. "We didn't use to see remote detonators and mercury switches, but now we do. They've started to use daisy chains—three or four IEDs linked together with detonator cord. They're getting terrorist help. Al Qaida."

Recalling how easy it was to cross into Iraq on this trip compared with my experience before the invasion, I explained that a lone Iraq Police officer barely scanned the back seat of our GMC before waving us from Jordan into Iraq. "Why are the borders so wide open? It's tougher to cross the U.S.–Canada border at Detroit," I said. Gwinner looked surprised to hear that and said, "That's a tough question." Recovering quickly, he added, "We're not trying to isolate Iraq. We're trying to rebuild it; to normalize trade."

I asked about the mass arrests his battalion made at the nearby village of Abu Siffa on the night of last December 16, specifically about the 14- and 15-year-olds and the sick elderly man villagers told me they had seen apprehended. Gwinner replied, "The ones I looked at were very healthy and a mean age in the early twenties. We don't detain children."

"What about the two houses the villagers told me your guys went back and destroyed on two later raids?"

"We didn't destroy them. They're still being inhabited. Maybe one was destroyed in a firefight. We found hundreds of pounds of explosives and detonators in that village," the Major countered. "Of course they'll tell you half the story or flat-out lie. It's not that we're cynical or anything," he smiled, and then used the same phrase I had heard Lieutenant Colonel Sassaman use to describe local residents, "it's just that they're all pathological liars."

"Look," Gwinner concluded, "even in Saddam Hussein's time it was known that people around here are crazy. They mortared the airbase near here after Saddam built it because he took some of their tribal land. They mortared their own airbase. They're crazy!"

Later that afternoon, sitting in the warm sunshine inside FOB Paliwoda, Tychostup and I interviewed Lieutenant Colonel Nathan Sassaman about his 11 months in Iraq leading some 800 officers and enlisted men and women.

"Soldiers are like all people, they can see right through their bosses," the former Army quarterback said in a brief response to a comment that morale seemed good and his leadership respected. He quickly changed the subject.

"We took 129 attacks from the area in and around Abu Hishma during the period from July to October 2003, some of which resulted in deaths and injuries. We met with some of the local sheiks, who insisted it was 'not us' behind the attacks, but it became apparent that it was. One morning we took eight mortar strikes all at once. Within two hours we got all eight of the mortars and a bunch of rounds that had been left near them."

Sassaman estimated the population in the area around Balad under his authority was about 180,000 with about 7,000 to 10,000 people living in Abu Hishma. "The people in that village are very different for some reason. Somebody terrorized that group of people . . . went around and said anyone caught working with the U.S. would be killed. Abu Hishma was the only place we got zero information or zero contacts."

"Coming up to Ramadan last fall, 4th Infantry said to pull back and let the ICDC (Iraq Civil Defense Corps, newly instituted and trained by U.S. forces) handle things. On November 17, they ambushed one of our patrols and killed Sgt. Panchot. I obviously was not getting their attention through meetings and door-to-door visits," Sassaman frowned.

"We needed to do something else. I do believe that controlled violence leads to fewer attacks. It took us two to three weeks to coordinate actions in response to the ambush that killed Sgt. Panchot," but since then there's been little or no violence, he asserted.

The battalion commander continued that "everywhere else villages were 'getting it;' other places around Balad, but not Abu Hishma. There just seems to be a hard line group here that sees us as occupiers." But he added that he'd reduced the number of fighters in that group to two, and was confident of getting the information needed to capture or kill them.

Asked how he obtained information on suspected resistance fighters, Sassaman replied that one way was to pay cash for it. "And the leaders (sheiks) for the most part don't want violence." He explained, "A group of farmers gave us information on some 40 people. We went down the list with them. Some were detained. Some weren't."

Asked how many detainees his troops had rounded up from Abu Hishma, Sassaman replied, "we haven't really kept track. I'd have to go back and check the records." He guessed that the total was around 100 to 150, some of whom had been released before being transferred to prisons.

I asked him about the same December 16 raid on Abu Siffa about which I had earlier quizzed Gwinner, in which eighty-three men, virtually all the males in the hamlet, were detained at 2:00 in the morning. According to residents of the village, the reason for the raid was to apprehend a man named Kais Hattam.

Sassaman agreed that Hattam was their target because his name appeared in Ba'ath Party documents found with Saddam Hussein who had been captured less than three days before the Abu Siffa raid. He described Hattam as a "key figure, one of five regional directors of the Ba'ath Party."

The Lieutenant Colonel's version of the raid was that seventy-three people, not eighty-three were rounded up, all adults. He said his men found a several-acre compound with a large quantity of material for making IEDs, weapons, and "just a ton of explosives." He added that three of the detainees were later released for health reasons.

Asked why so many villagers were rounded up after the Army got the man they were looking for, he replied that the amount of weapons and explosives implicated Abu Siffa as a center of resistance, further proven by the fact that his base had been mortared from that area.

"We still need one more 'communication' with the hardcore attackers to get their attention. That group at Abu Hishma has just never accepted that we want to help them," he added, asserting that, "You get their attention through controlled violence" along with money for infrastructure projects.

Earlier, I had asked Sassaman if he regretted a frequently cited comment he made to the *New York Times:* "With a heavy dose of fear and violence, and a lot of money for projects, I think we can convince these people that we are here to help them." He smiled grimly and said it had been a "bad day" when he spoke with *Times* reporter, Dexter Filkins.

"I'm convinced that Iraqis want peace, or let me say, they want to go back to normal tribal violence, but most Iraqis don't want constant war. Kids don't want to be soldiers. They want to be teachers. And I want them to be teachers," Sassaman concurred, although he added that "kids as young as fifteen have taken up weapons against us. They're offered a hundred dollars for firing an RPG at us and some respond."

When I told Sassaman that I had heard many comments from Iraqis against encircling Abu Hishma with miles of razor wire, he stoutly defended its effectiveness, claiming the villagers feel it is as much for their own safety as the Army's.

"I've walked the streets of Abu Hishma countless times and I always ask 'should I take the wire down?' They always respond, 'no, not yet.'" He claimed the village residents believe the fence keeps resistance fighters from using their orange groves as places from which to launch mortar attacks, thereby eliminating the need for his troops to strike back.

"I'm not interested in winning hearts and minds here," Sassaman said. We're here to provide security and safety. We're interested in respect."
At the end of the interview, Sassaman reflected on his time spent in the Balad area.

"We really have come to help," he said. "One of the most frustrating things is having to deal with the attacks."

Lieutenant Colonel Sassaman said that he holds a Master's degree in Public Administration, but from his experience in Iraq he has learned that "I don't want to be a city manager in any city large or small—I did my doctoral work here."

He explained that after he took command of the area, he held a series of meetings to determine the local residents' priorities. "They said they wanted health clinics and roads, so that's what we did. Today we opened the surgical wing at Balad Hospital. You don't hear much about that in the news, though." He said road repair was less of a success because the first contractor they paid to resurface an important roadway had barely started the job and "disappeared with our $30,000. That's life in Iraq." A new contractor was hired and resurfacing had begun.

"In retrospect, we probably should have started with our priorities—security and water. But, being Americans, we wanted them to develop their own priorities and that's what we went with.

"Saddam built a large middle class," Sassaman observed, "but they were too dependent on the central government. Now we've got a case of too much freedom, too fast. They didn't earn it themselves; an outside force did it for them. They didn't pay the price of gaining a republic. My advice is, next time you have a dictator for thirty-five years, don't wait for an outside force to get rid of him."

Asked what he had learned from Iraqi people during his tour, Sassaman thought for a moment and replied, "The strength of their families. You have to look high and low in the U.S. to see families as tight. Here everyone pitches in, even the kids. Women's rights, though, is light years behind us."
"I think this is a good time for new units to come in. We've gone through a period of guerilla warfare and now it's secure and safe . . . the new units can help them progress much faster now. I've got high hopes. I'd like to come back and see this place—maybe in ten years. We're OK here up to June 30 (2004, the day the U.S. was scheduled to return "sovereignty" to Iraqis). But after that, every day we're here is a bad day," Sassaman concluded.

17

AN UNCOMMON MOM

What is the most common thing moms do? Take care of their kids?

That's what Susan Galleymore was doing when I met her. The uncommon thing was that she'd traveled halfway around the world, from San Francisco to Baghdad, to take care of her son. Nick is a U.S. Army Ranger, an occupation generally regarded as pretty rugged, or at least not likely to require a mother's personal touch. But that was not about to stop this committed former South African.

Now living in California, Galleymore became familiar with Post-Traumatic Stress Disorder (PTSD) when her brothers served in the South African Army during the "Front-line States" wars that nation waged against neighboring countries. "I know what PTSD is," she said, and added with a mother's steely resolve, "I'm not going to lose my son to that."

Over many glasses of tea at a Karrada Street café in central Baghdad, Galleymore described her anxiousness for her son, and her Internet project, called "Motherspeak," relating the anxieties of mothers on all sides of the Iraq war.

M Ferner (MF): You spoke earlier of an Iraqi mother whose whole family was killed in a tragic encounter with the U.S. military, and how that tragedy will ripple beyond what we might normally consider.

Susan Galleymore (SG): Yes, I spoke with an Iraqi woman whose husband and three children were killed. They were driving after dark in their neighborhood, visiting family. A humvee came around the corner about the time that an electrical transformer apparently exploded. Her husband tried telling the soldiers not to shoot, that he was with his family, but they were killed and she was wounded.

That is a horrible story. But my concern is also with the young soldiers in that position, where you do something because you're so scared and you can never find your way through it psychologically. And that's just one incident out of a whole plethora of things that are happening to these soldiers all the time. I'm really, really concerned about that aspect of my son. It's pretty scary. This is supposed to be a job. But it's a job with real, real consequences. Even though he's an adult, I can't let go. I can't not do what I can, to somehow work with him around that stuff. My son is not going to break down and open up to me about how terrible it was. He has a lot to defend because he knows I didn't really want him in the military. So given that, I have to find another way of supporting him.

The first American mom I interviewed had been a peacenik during the 60s. She married a man who was a Vietnam vet, in the 82nd (Airborne). Their son, who is nineteen, came straight out of boot camp to Iraq and he's in the 82nd. The son calls home every week. Every now and again he'll ask to speak privately to his dad and the two of them will talk through some experience that he's had. That was such a wonderful role for a father to be able to play in his son's life. My son's father can't really play that role, and I don't really know any men who can play that role for my son. So I sent a letter to that father who'd been in Vietnam and asked him if he'd make contact with Nicholas. Not to be overt about it, but just say that he'd been in the military and understands how harsh it gets. So I'm trying to find all these avenues, hoping that one of them may spark something for Nicholas.

MF: What are you hoping it will spark?

SG: That instead of holding a severely difficult, traumatic experience inside, he'll be able to bring it out and talk about it and see that this is something that goes along with the territory and that people can actually talk about it; that men actually talk about it. It's not something they hold inside all the time—which is my impression of the way men are. They tend not to be overtly open about that sort of stuff. I don't want that to happen to him. I want him to find a way to bring it out within the manly culture.

So far, the American mothers I've talked to, except for the first mother who's married to the Vietnam vet, I think, have not really taken on the responsibility of the mental health of their kids. They're still thinking the military will do it. One of the people I talked with here is a psychiatrist working with post-traumatic stress in little kids and he also works with the CPA (Coalition Provisional Authority, the body administering U.S. authority over Iraq), with the soldiers. But he said it's so minimal that it's almost non-existent. If it's not expedient they don't bother. So, I decided I'm not going to watch my kid disappear into this war and not do my best to find another track for him. It ain't gonna happen.

MF: Many parents, if they thought about it, would have the same concerns that you do, but probably not many of them would travel here from California to do something about it. What made you decide to travel halfway around the world to visit your son?

SG: I know I'm in a weird position, not wanting to interfere with my son's choices but understanding that the ones he made are really dangerous. I wasn't going to tell him that … I'm just trying to get a sense of where he's at. I'm not going to ask him, "how are you, dear, and is everything ok?" He's a little annoyed for me being here, so we may have to get over that hump, but I would prefer just to talk about basic, ordinary stuff. My concern is that when he gets out of here in six months, besides the physical health problems he's facing, I hope I'm wrong, but I believe he'll be dealing with some heavy-duty psychological stuff.

When Nick was in Afghanistan, I tried to think of a project we could work on together, expecting he would be coming out of the military this July, but he re-upped for three more years. I was thinking he'd need some kind of decompression time and maybe we could work on a project together—maybe two voices of war—a mother and son sort of thing. It would be interesting and maybe it would be a way to work through some of the things in his head. When he came to visit after he got out of Afghanistan, I realized this was not going to happen at this time. But I was not giving up on my target that my kid is not gonna disappear if I can help it. Then when they sent him to Iraq, I was furious because they had promised he would return home for Special Forces training. So I said, "look, if I'm having this much trouble with (what's going on in) Iraq, there are definitely a whole host of mothers who wake up at 3 o'clock in the morning, panicked about what's happening with their kids." I'm really curious about where those mothers are coming from. Some of them are really gung-ho, saying "my son is fighting for the country," and others are like, "well, I didn't want him to go, but he's there." I'm really interested in finding those voices . . . not from an ideological perspective, but sort of find out what it's like for a parent to have a kid over here and hear about these bombings and every time you turn on the television there's another dead soldier—and wondering if it's your kid.

From there I thought, "Well that would be interesting, but what would be really interesting would be the other side of it," you know, because we get so little news about Iraq. We get the sort of chewed up and digested version that's spit out on the other end that says, "Oh, ok, George Bush is doing a great job." And I know that isn't true. So I knew this would be a dangerous environment but it wouldn't be half as dangerous as they were portraying, and I decided to come and check it out and get that other viewpoint. I mean, George Bush actually says the Iraqis are not our enemy . . . and I'm taking him at his word for once (laughs).

MF: What about your background got you started in this direction?

SG: I grew up in apartheid South Africa. I grew up in the country and my parents had a hotel. I had nannies and cooks and some very close relationships with them, in a lot of cases closer than with my parents. They took care of me and I grew up with them. Then when I was about fourteen, I came into contact with the whole notion of the holocaust and war. I read a lot about it and I read a lot about how people were injured by it. They called it shell-shocked in those days. Then my brothers went into the military. My older brother was in an area near what was Angola at the time. South Africa was conducting a war that would later be called the war against the "front-line states," but internally within South Africa there was no war. No one talked about it as a war. It was called "doing your army training on the border." In the meantime, South Africa was doing incursions and massacring people in Botswana and Angola and the South African public didn't know about it. My brother was in that and he told me a couple stories that are still really really hard for me to talk about because they were so vile. He's fifty now and he's just sort of broken through the cloud. We don't talk about the war, although I had talked about my concerns for Nicholas, and he said, "Oh, Nicholas is doing what he wants, he's having a great time. Leave him alone."

So I don't know where this concern came from. I'm just very aware of what psychological health is and what it isn't, and what it can do to you to hurt or kill or maim or humiliate other people and have it sanctioned at a high level.

MF: You mentioned not wanting your son to "get lost." What would getting lost consist of?

SG: It could consist of a lot of different things. In San Francisco, there are a lot of street people at various levels of being in touch with reality and it happens to be true that a lot of those folks are Vietnam vets. The system failed those people and they don't have anyone else on their side rooting for them. That's kind of a really harsh level of this, and my kid ain't gonna go that direction. I don't believe he would, but there are various other levels of functionality. He could fall into various other traps, I think.

MF: Do you mean drugs?

SG: No, he's not a drug guy. I've heard of sort of spontaneous outbursts of violence in the family—those sort of things. My son doesn't drink much and he doesn't smoke, so I'd be surprised if he did get into drugs, but that's always a possibility. Looking at the whole range of things that could happen to him . . . the worst one being a street person at sort of a higher functioning level and being too ashamed of himself to be with anyone.

MF: Has he told you whether he's been in firefights or seen any casualties?

SG: He was in eastern Afghanistan and I know they went out on patrols and he saw some of his buddies killed . . . not killed by hostile fire, but killed by drunken driving accidents and stupid accidents like that. But it could not be as bad as it is here. Of course, there were civilians under occupation there, but where they were it was so isolated.

It's a weird thing, when he came back from Afghanistan, I was very ginger around him, because I wanted to get those details but I didn't want to seem sort of bloodthirsty, so I was kind of waiting for these things to emerge in sort of an organic way. I didn't want to just sit down and say, "OK, have you killed anyone, or who have you seen killed?" That just seemed really crude to me. But once I invited my girlfriend to dinner, and she didn't have any of those parental hesitations and she just asked him straight out. He was really happy and open to talk about it. He told us about a kid that was in the turret of a humvee and when it tipped over he was crushed to death . . . and he was due to go home in two days.

And then there was the story about how the soldiers, in this very masculine environment—camouflage, trucks, there's no softness there, there's no flowers, it's just bleak—and someone brought in a rabbit to eat. They didn't eat it but it became their pet. And some dogs from the neighborhood sort of wandered in and became pets. And then an order came down that all the dogs had to be shot. What for? I don't know, but this is the way it is. The colonel said, "We don't have pets on base." So they had to go out and shoot the dogs . . . you know that's like shooting your friend. The guys had gone through the whole thing, they spayed and neutered the dogs and then they were told to shoot them. Nicholas shot one through the neck but it wasn't killed, so they fixed it . . . but then they had to shoot it again later. So those kinds of stories I've heard, but we haven't gotten into the really nitty gritty stuff. Some of it was that I was afraid . . . afraid of hearing how damaged he was already after just six months. Then I understood that it was my fear and that wasn't very helpful to him, and that he was in a real hellhole now, and I decided it was enough about me. It wasn't about my fear hearing something bad; it was about my son's actual reality.

MF: In the book, *Achilles in Vietnam,* the author, Jonathan Shay, explains that society asks soldiers to do terrible things, and that whether or not soldiers readily reintegrate into society is based in part on whether people back home will want to hear about their experiences. Is that something you've thought about in relation to your son?

SG: The way I see it is how isolated you have to be with your actions—if society is open to hearing about it then you're less isolated and maybe you can talk about it some night over a beer and maybe it escalates into sort of a confession. Or if society is really against it, then you'd have to hold it close and be really guarded. One of the mothers I interviewed related the story of a kid, eighteen years old, who shot his first person over here and he just crumpled . . . just couldn't take it and they sent him back home. He said, "Yeah, it wasn't like a video game at all. When I saw that person actually fall down, I realized what I'd done."

What can we do about this? It's so shameful the way we deal with these folks and what's put upon them. The whole thing is shameful. I've been the loudmouth, pushy person out on the barricades and I'm just not there anymore. It's such a huge task. I want to work in a way that gets things to happen, one small step at a time, starting with just my son. I invite other mothers to do the same.

18

THE ALBANIAN MAFIA AND OTHER STORIES FROM CIRCUS 2 IRAQ

AGADIR HOTEL, BAGHDAD

Sitting on the floor of room 412 in this 1.5-star *fenduk* in central Baghdad, sipping a beer, and swatting the occasional cockroach, Peter Simms graciously corrected his host. "I'm a professional fool, not a clown. There is a difference, you know."

With a twinkle in his eye, the long-haired, lanky, ex-soldier introduced me to Circus 2 Iraq, a troupe of five clowns and entertainers from England, France, and Australia who'd come to provide kids in this war-torn country with a measure of joy and respite.

I watched them charm the neighborhood kids near their apartment building dubbed "The Clown House," off Karrada Street, and perform in a wretched squatter camp outside of town. But that night I wanted to learn how he got into that line of work. How did this curious band come to be? To my good fortune, he began, in a thick working-class British accent, with the story of the Albanian mafia.

You know in Albania, guns are everything. Besides that, it's easy to offend someone and get a blood feud going that will last almost forever. Well I knew these two neighbors who were feuding over something or other and got their own little arms race going. The first fellow bought a knife. So his neighbor got a machete. The first fellow then gets a pistol and his neighbor buys a Kalashnikov. Then the first guy responds with an RPG. The neighbor is not to be outdone, so he buys a MIG fighter. A MIG fighter! He doesn't know how to fly it! He has no ammunition for it if he did! But he can say, 'I've got a MIG sitting in my back yard and you're not going to mess with me!'

So that tells you something important about Albania.

Well I finds m'self in Albania a few years ago, working for this British NGO that's teaching 'minor weapons awareness' to children. This is no trifling matter when you consider that there are more small arms in Albania than there are grandparents. My job was to go to schools and use a bit 'o magic and some foolery to entertain the kids, and at the same time teach them not to play with guns.

Well, in Albania, you can't even talk about guns without the mafia taking notice of you. So it was one night, about 10 o'clock, I gets a knock on the door. I opened it up, and there stands four guys in black leather jackets and sunglasses—at 10 o'clock at night. So I guess right away they're the mafia.

Now in Albania, they have a wonderful custom. If you invite a guest into your home, they cannot kill you, because you are a gift from God. So of course, the first thing I do when I see these four gentlemen is say, 'please come in and sit down.' So they did.

The leader of the group takes off his sunglasses and says to me, 'Now we know what you're doing here in our town, talking to the children about guns, and we came here to tell you that you have our total respect. We support you 100 percent.'

Glad to hear this, I was, so I smiled and said, 'thank you.' And then he did the oddest thing. He pulled a bullet out of 'is pocket and hands it to me. And he explained that now he can't kill me, because he's just given me the bullet that he would have killed me with. 'This is quite a nice custom,' I says to m'self.

So we sat there and talked for a while and I asked them if they'd like something to drink. They said they might, and I poured them a shot. And we talked for a while more, and had another shot. Then we talked and had another shot, and had another shot and talked some more.

Pretty soon, he looks at me and says, 'How'd you like to come up to our lodge this weekend?'

Well, I couldn't think of anything better, so I said, 'sure.'

So about 4 o'clock on Friday afternoon, when I'm finished with my last talk at the school, a brand new BMW pulls up at the front of the building and the driver motions me in. We go tearing off, and pretty soon, we're up into the mountains, zipping around curves . . . just flying along. Before long, we stop at a beautiful lodge with just the grandest view of the valley below, and he says, 'Here we are!'

I look around at the view for a few seconds and go in to meet me mates. We shake hands, say hello, and someone gets out a bottle. Well, let's just say that before long we're all pretty well pissed.

The next thing I know, my friend who gave me the bullet puts down 'is glass, looks at me and asks, 'You want to go shoot some guns?' Now I ask you, how do you tell the mafia no, you'd rather not go shoot guns? So of course I said yes.

We go outside, down a lane near the lodge, and one of the guys hands me a gun and says, 'Here, try this.' Boom! I take a shot at a tree in the distance. Then he hands me another one, and another one, and pretty soon, I'm shooting I don't know what sort of guns—bigger than anything I'd ever seen in the British Army! BOOM! And there goes part of a mountain! We had the greatest fun!

And that was the weekend—shooting guns and drinking—all weekend! So here it comes, Monday morning bright and early, and I've got to go back to work. My mafia friend drives me back down to the school in the village, and

Pete and Luis, two members of "Circus 2 Iraq," perform for an audience of children at Baghdad's National Theater. (*Photo by Mike Ferner*)

I walk in, stinking of gunpowder and alcohol, telling the kiddies, 'DON'T play with guns, and DON'T mess with the mafia.'

It's the God's truth, and it's how I got connected with people who got me to Iraq!

♦ ♦ ♦

SHA'A LE SQUATTER'S CAMP

Although some journalists eagerly anticipate "embedding" with the 82nd Airborne, or the 3rd Marines, my job one day was to accompany a troupe of clowns and fools, the Circus 2 Iraq, on a trip to perform for the kids of Sha'a Le squatter's camp.

To reach this northwest corner of Baghdad one drove through a district of impromptu curbside markets that spilled onto both sides of the road and all over the median in between. Sheep, goats, chickens, and cows stood cheek-by-jowl with portable slaughtering stations, manure piles, swirls of dust, lambs grazing in trash heaps, and kids darting everywhere. The aroma brought me dangerously close to losing my breakfast.

Our destination was an abandoned, state-run poultry farm, "home" to over a hundred families, including 700 children—a truly miserable spot of dirt and concrete with two water taps and no sewers. Its sole advantage was

In one of the dozen squatter camps established in Baghdad after the Saddam Hussein government was toppled, women make flatbread in a small cement-block oven. (*Photo by Mike Ferner*)

One of many tents that provide shelter in a Baghdad squatter camp. (*Photo by Mike Ferner*)

that shortly after the Hussein government fell in April 2003, it became a free place to live. Pila Hassan was the camp's leader.

Preparing for a matinee performance, Uzma, Peter, and Jo, from the United Kingdom, and Luis, from France, shared a small, vacant building for a dressing room. Luis was the first out and was immediately mobbed by forty

With no plumbing or sewage system, water stands in the front yard of a home in a Baghdad squatter camp. (*Photo by Mike Ferner*)

or fifty kids, most of whom had blood-red hands that startled me until I learned it was from the henna they were playing with. Soon Jo and Uzma appeared and the parachute games began.

Circus 2 Iraq's routines had to be both entertaining and inexpensive to produce. That's what made "Parachute Cat and Mouse" a staple. The kids held the edge of the red, round nylon fabric and waved it up and down close to the ground. The "mouse" ran wildly on top of the chute, eluding the "cat," who ran frantically in pursuit beneath the cloth. Within seconds, the air filled with screamed directions to predator and prey, and shrieks of pure delight.

The heat and dust made for a very quick game of Paracat-and-mouse, but the kids paid the elements no heed. Jo introduced the next game, one that required teamwork all around the parachute to keep a large red ball in the air without touching it.

Partway through that game, Pete invited me to tour the camp with Hassan.

The shouts of joy faded as we walked around the back of the building. We observed a small earthen oven for baking flatbread and next to that, a communal water tap. Water from it drained slowly towards the camp perimeter. Pete pointed to a large, stagnant pool less than fifty feet away and said that's how far the water went in about a week.

Next stop on the tour was a cement-block building that used to be the slaughterhouse. Cement trusses provided the only "roof." Three families lived within the walls. One family lived in a tiny, one-room brick structure that was substantial only in relation to the rest of the camp housing, which was built mostly of reeds and cardboard. The floor boasted a small, colorful rug. Two magazine pictures graced the walls.

Because of the location, the slaughterhouse families had a cement floor. But just beyond them stretched a wide-open space where a mother, father, and three children lived in a reed and cloth tent, with a dirt floor. The view out their front entrance was of an area the size of a narrow city lot, flooded with several inches of fetid water from a thunderstorm ten days ago.

The camp "supermarket" was next on the tour. A small cement-block room, it contained two shelves holding a couple of dozen cans of food and a few dry goods. A lone clerk sat at a card table and managed a smile as we stopped in to look.

Further on, a donkey dozed inside the perimeter of a former building's foundation. The structure that replaced it consisted of one brick wall and three walls of reeds and corrugated metal. To its left stood a unit of new construction, consisting of about 100 square feet of living space framed by two reed arches and crisscrossed reed supports. We said "Sa'alam a lekum," to several children peering at us from behind it. Our greetings were met with atypical silence and stares. Hassan related sadly that none of the family could hear or speak.

He pointed out a concrete pad on the ground with no walls or roof, referring to it as their former school that they hoped to rebuild.

Back at the one-room brick home in the former slaughterhouse, Hassan invited us to have lunch with him at the nearby home of Kamis Hammed. After apologies were made for "such simple fare," we were served a lunch of warm flatbread, lamb, and vegetables, followed by tea.

Bravely trying out his limited English, Pila Hassan told us a little about the people of Sha'a Le. Many were displaced from the south of Iraq where they lived off fish and game. Others came from small towns and some from Baghdad itself, during and immediately after the U.S. invasion. "In Iraq, we have 35 years of war . . . wars with Iran, Kuwait, the U.S. In Iraq there is money for scuds (missiles), bombs and TNT, but the schools are dirty. The people are dirty."

After lunch, we thanked Mr. Hammed and exited his one-room home into bright sunshine bouncing off concrete. With great deference, we were shown a sink with running water where we could wash our hands. Half-a-dozen pigeons walked tamely past us, looking for bits of food on the floor.

On our way back to the performance, several children accompanied us, asking to have their picture taken. A young girl holding her baby sister with two younger brothers in tow, all had streaks of red in their black hair, and henna-red fingers.

We arrived at the circus just in time for the closing act. Uzma and Luis were pantomiming a story about a mean boss and a street sweeper more interested in dancing with a whimsical box that plays music whenever the lid opened. The boss finally has his way and smashes the box. In the final scene, Uzma carefully picked up the pieces and placed them tearfully in a trash bin. To her delight and the riotous cheers of her audience, music started coming out of the trash bin as she wheeled it away. Joy remained triumphant!

After the show, Pete appeared wearing his fool's cap and curled pointy shoes, Luis and Uzma reappeared as boss and sweeper, and Jo emerged on her stilts, blowing bubbles, accompanied by Mr. Hassan for a brief, closing ceremony.

When Circus 2 Iraq had performed in Sha'a Le once before, they had immediately seen the deplorable living conditions. Members of the troupe had emailed an appeal to friends in Britain to raise the £300 needed to install a drainpipe from the stagnant pool to a nearby stream. After this most recent show, Jo handed the money to a beaming Mr. Hassan, whose reply gave Circus 2 Iraq something to cheer about in return—he had already spoken with a contractor who was ready to do the work.

So ended a typical day for a most atypical bunch of clowns and fools.

19

COPS AND CLOWNS

The unfailing hospitality of the Middle East assured an invitation to the party, even though I'd been a neighbor across the hall for barely forty-eight hours and had yet to even meet the guest of honor—a resident of the "clown flat" in the narrow, three-story apartment building off Karrada Street in central Baghdad.

It started innocently enough. Someone handed me a beer as I sat down on the long, blue shag carpet that looked and smelled like it had been installed in King Hammurabi's reign. A quick look around the tiny living room and the adjoining kitchen, bath, and bedroom explained why the rent was so reasonable. The air was thick with "character." Alcohol was legal to serve in private homes, but I wondered about the sweet-smelling smoke rising out of the *nargila* being imbibed in the corner.

Listening to a mix of Arabic, cockney English, Australian English, and French, I watched two clowns throw a dollop of light back and forth, completely unprepared for the next scene.

Through the open doorway strode three Iraqi police: a young lieutenant carrying a sidearm and two younger sergeants shouldering AK-47s, escorting a hapless youth who was talking in highly animated American English. The party continued, but a small knot of people gathered to listen. What followed was something I feel safe in saying would never, *ever* be witnessed in the United States.

The young American, an exchange student from a New England college attending school in Egypt, had come to Baghdad to visit a British friend living upstairs from the clown flat where the party was being held. At the young American's insistence, the police brought him home so he could find his passport and papers needed to prove he was working as a journalist when he was arrested the night before.

It seems that his British friend, still sitting in jail, had gone out on a graffiti mission with a can of spray paint, and the student/journalist had gone out to cover the activity. That part was a bit shaky, as his press "credentials" consisted of a letter from the journalism department of his school back in New England.

I was in no position to be judgmental about credentials since all I had were letters from editors at *Rolling Stone,* the *New Hampshire Gazette,* and *Pacific News Service* saying noncommittally, "We'll take a look at what you send us." My press pass from the National Writers Union was due to arrive any day, but in the meantime all I could muster was a scrawny notebook and my best journalistic bearing as I began taking notes furiously. One young man had already started filming the event with a camcorder.

The student's letter from journalism school began to look more and more like a desperately grabbed straw. His claim to journalistic immunity, even when made through Ahmad, a sympathetic translator, was not gaining much traction with the police. And if he couldn't make a reasonable argument for why he had accompanied the spray painter, he was headed back to jail.

It should be mentioned here that the conversation among police, student, Ahmad, and various bystanders was not only remarkably civil but, in a strange way, incredibly more humane, even humorous, than you could ever imagine in a similar scene in the United States. More than once, the police were ready to escort the student back to jail, but waited to hear one more bystander's argument.

Unlike what I expected in such a situation, the police were amazingly patient. The young sergeants even had a hard time hiding occasional smiles. Still, I sensed an air of foreboding. It felt like things could go bad, and quickly. Thinking that more "press presence" might help keep things cool, I decided to take a more active role and asked the officers for their names. Too late, I realized my mistake.

One of the sergeants tried to determine what I had asked. To be helpful, I pointed to the ID tag hanging around his neck. He said the Arabic equivalent of "oh, sure," and started to show me the tag. The lieutenant yanked the tag out of his hand, turned it to the blank side, and quickly did the same with his own and the other sergeant's ID. Ahmad clearly did not need to repeat in English, "NO NAMES."

Belatedly, I tried something reassuring, which turned out to be, "Oh, it's nothing. Don't worry, it's just standard practice to get everyone's name." That didn't seem to help much. The culture of repression every Iraqi in the room had known since birth, the fact that their government had been overthrown less than a year earlier by the same nation I was from, and the fact that the police likely had no training for such situations—all added up to a sensitive situation.

Doing considerably more to keep things cool than my lame attempt to get police officers' names, a young woman standing on a pair of stilts blew streams of bubbles through the air. As they drifted down toward the police, the sergeants reached up to catch them. The lieutenant was less amused, but seeing smiles on the faces of several people involved in the procedure had a calming, humanizing effect. The small, iridescent spheres floating through the air even seemed to encourage the police to be more patient.

"What is he being charged with?" the stilts clown asked, blowing more bubbles. "You know, you have to have some kind of charge if you're going to arrest this man."

More bubbles.

Finally, the lieutenant determined that despite shaky credentials, a dozen arguments, a room full of interested bystanders, a bubble-blowing clown on stilts, and two instant journalists, the young man had to return to jail.

"Well, if he's going, we're all going," another clown hollered, to which everyone, even the police, agreed! From there it was a scramble down the stairs to see who would ride in the back of the Iraqi Police's small Mitsubishi pickup and who might have a car. Probably more out of deference to my grey hair than to my journalistic demeanor, everyone insisted I take the passenger bench in the cab with one of the sergeants, who seemed to be particularly enjoying this unlikely evening.

What followed was a truly madcap trip through deserted central Baghdad, lights flashing, spraying our way through deep pools of standing water and sewage, careening around curves much faster than necessary by anyone's measure, and people nearly bouncing out of the trucks, all of which is recorded on film somewhere.

Arriving at a most somber-looking, deserted intersection, we turned and headed straight for a police station. It was easy to imagine Saddam Hussein's police taking a prisoner here who might never be heard from again, or a family of Iraqis detained at 2:00 A.M. by U.S. troops, approaching this same jail. It felt very strange to be part of such a party-like atmosphere, protected in large part by our Westernness, pulling up to that police station. There was a very good chance we would be able to walk away, unlike so many before us.

Inside, the dim light and jail cells quickly produced a more sober mood, even before the night duty officers made their appearance. Gruffer, bigger, older, these guys did *not* look like they wanted to see any bubbles and they did not want to have a gaggle of supporters and journalists clogging the hallway, cheering on the student and his partner in crime. We were told to leave.

Part of the group started to edge toward the exit. The other part didn't budge. Blocked from my view, I heard a young British voice shout, "You cannot hold these men without charges! It is against international law! If you do, you are no better than the last regime!"

I moved to see Jo Wilding, the bubbling stilt clown of just twenty minutes ago, standing implacably in the hallway, now much shorter and with a dead serious look on her face. She repeated her warning and everyone stopped.

"We aren't leaving unless these guys come with us," someone shouted.

"No, you are leaving. And you're leaving right now," a police officer demanded in return.

"Guys, I really think it's time to go . . . seriously," Ahmad added quickly, and most of the bunch continued on its way to the exit, except Jo, who demanded to talk with the officer in charge.

To my amazement, the police agreed to talk with her as long as the rest of the delegation moved back and stood silently. Within two minutes, Jo, Ahmad, and the ranking officer reached an agreement. The two young men would be released the very first thing in the rapidly approaching morning, and we were to go home. No one was entirely comfortable with the arrangement, but it was the best we were going to get. With that, and many calls of "We'll be back in the morning," the clowns and the police parted company.

The Iraqi police released the prisoners the next day.

20

SPRINGTIME IN FALLUJAH

The incidents described in this story happened about three weeks after I returned home on March 15, 2004 from my second trip. They are the only incidents in this book that I did not personally witness, but were witnessed by two people you have read about, Jo Wilding and Dahr Jamail. What follows is taken largely from Wilding's email dispatches of that period, with her permission. I include it because it is one of the very few independent, eyewitness accounts of one of the most critical operations carried out by the U.S. military during the war on Iraq.

The following quote attributed to Jesuit priest, Daniel Berrigan, is a favorite among peace activists: "We will only achieve success when we show the same courage for peace as soldiers do for war." In April of 2004, in Fallujah, a small band of friends did exactly that.

Few places in Iraq resented and resisted the U.S. occupation more than residents of this city of 300,000. In one incident on March 29, 2004, a large group of people gathered at a school occupied by U.S. troops to demand they leave. Soldiers fired into the crowd, killing seventeen civilians. Two days later, at a rally protesting those killings, troops again opened fire on the crowd and killed three more people.

The Fallujahns' next response was violent, killing four U.S. mercenaries employed by Blackwater USA Corporation and hanging their bodies from a bridge over the Euphrates River. The U.S. military responded with massive force in what became known as the first siege of Fallujah.

Refugees from Fallujah quickly began arriving in Baghdad. They described an around-the-clock nightmare of what some have labeled war crimes committed by the U.S. military: bombing hospitals, killing civilians carrying white flags, running over the wounded with tanks, and bodies piling up so fast the soccer field had to be turned into a cemetery.

Jo Wilding was part of a dozen people—Iraqis, assorted internationals, and journalists—who determined they had to do something. She described how a journalist friend of hers, Leigh Gordon and his friend Ghareeb, "turned up at my door at about 11pm the night of April 9, telling me things were desperate in

Fallujah. He'd been bringing out children with their limbs blown off . . . aid vehicles and the media were being turned away . . . "

She learned that some Italian medical NGOs had contributed medical supplies and " . . . there was a better chance of it getting there with foreigners, Westerners, to get through the American checkpoints." The group decided to take in a bus with supplies, see what else they could do, and then bring people out on the bus who needed to leave.

"Although I was far from confident that we could do it, I knew if we didn't, no one else could even have a chance . . . if we didn't try to help them, no one would."

Early in the afternoon of April 10, this seat-of-the-pants relief mission traveled from Baghdad to Fallujah in two vehicles, taking backroads to avoid U.S. checkpoints. A lead car driven by an Iraqi man carried the nephew of a local sheikh and a guide who cleared their passage through resistance fighters' checkpoints. The bus with medical supplies followed, driven by the son of the car driver. As they passed through small towns off the main road between Baghdad and Fallujah, people at makeshift refreshment stands waved and threw food for them and the people they were going to assist, Jo recalled.

The thirty-year-old native of Bristol, England, kept a journal of those days and published reports on the Internet. Those accounts described what she saw in the killing ground of Fallujah in the spring of 2004.

When the emergency mission reached Fallujah, their guides took them to a makeshift aid station in the part of town not controlled by the Americans. Fallujahns immediately opened the boxes of supplies. Blankets were most popular since linens of any kind to cover the bloody gurneys were in short supply. Jo described the grim conditions. "It's not a hospital at all but a private doctor's surgery (office) treating people free since air strikes destroyed the town's main hospital." At another makeshift clinic in a car garage, there was no anesthetic, and doctors took blood bags out of a drinks fridge before warming them up under the tap in a dirty bathroom.

In the makeshift clinic, Jo saw an old woman with a bullet wound in her abdomen. The bed under her foot was blood-soaked from another wound. She still clutched a white flag in her hand. Jo said the story she told was the same one she'd heard from other Fallujahns: she was leaving her home in the U.S.-controlled part of the city to flee to Baghdad when a sniper shot her. The old woman and others who told Jo similar stories were adamant the snipers were U.S. Marines.

"The electricity in Fallujah has been off for days and when the generator runs out of petrol they just have to manage," she wrote. When the electric generator sputtered to a halt, so did the lights in the makeshift operating room. Someone held up a cigarette lighter so the doctor could continue, "but," Jo observed, "the children he's working on are not going to live."

"The snipers are not only taking a toll on the people but on the ambulance, too," Jo recorded. "It has been shot up and repaired four times already."

Bodies lay in the streets because no one could collect them without also being shot.

Throwing what little caution they'd exercised till then to the wind, Jo and her fellow Samaritans borrowed a pickup truck to bring in the wounded. In that mad situation, they reasoned that such a vehicle might be less likely to be shot. Even desperate Fallujahns told them it was the craziest thing they'd ever seen.

Into the silent fright of the no man's land between resistance fighters and Marines, the rescuers slowly drove their truck. Around a corner, a woman opened the gate of her home and pointed down the street to a man lying in a gutter near a car. Jo could also see two Marines less than 100 feet away, but wasn't sure they could see her, so at the top of her voice she bellowed, "HELLO. CAN YOU HEAR ME?"

From the silence so thick "you could hear the flies buzzing at 50 paces," she got no response. "We are a medical team. We want to move this wounded man. Is it OK? Can you give us a signal that it's OK?"

After repeated attempts to get a response, including one from another volunteer with an American accent, they got permission. Raising their hands, they walked toward the man lying in the gutter. He wore a blue and black striped football shirt with a big "28" on the back. A cloud of flies and a hot, sour smell greeted them. A Kalashnikov was attached to his hand with sticky blood, so Jo put her foot on the rifle as they picked up his shoulders, watching as " . . . his blood falls out through the hole in his back. We heave him into the pickup as best we can and try to outrun the flies."

The next afternoon the ambulance was back in service, taking more volunteers on a similar mission. With the lights and siren on, Jo, the visible Westerner and therefore the team's "passport," sat in the front seat by the passenger window.

Suddenly, a bullet crashed through the ambulance and the driver immediately stopped. He turned off the siren but kept the blue light flashing. Jo and her companions kept their eyes on the U.S. Marines on the buildings. When the Marines fired several more shots, everyone in the ambulance ducked. Then more shots hit the ambulance. Of all possible responses, Jo started to sing. "What else do you do when someone's shooting at you," she asked herself. But when one of the shots blew out a tire and another took out the radiator, she got outraged. They'd been prevented from reaching their patient, a woman giving birth at home.

Darkness put an end to their mission as the ambulance limped back to the clinic. The ambulance was again out of commission and, with no light, the Marines wouldn't be able to see their foreign faces, further lessening their safety margins. Jo wrote, "The acting director of the clinic says he hated Saddam but now he hates the Americans more."

A nearby explosion tore the air behind the building across the street. Within minutes a car roared up to the clinic and Jo heard the man screaming. " . . . there's no skin left on his body. He's burned from head to foot . . . He'll die of dehydration within a few days."

One of the haggard doctors at the clinic told Jo that in the last week he'd gotten only eight hours sleep, and missed the funerals of his brother and aunt because his skills were needed. "The dead we cannot help. I must worry about the injured."

Going out the next day in the pickup again, the Iraqi–British–U.S. team carried a white flag with a red crescent spray painted on it and soon ran into another unit of Marines, stationed on the rooftop of a home.

They held up the flag and shouted to the soldiers, two of whom came down to talk with them. The Marines asked Rana, an Iraqi woman with the team, to go into the house on which they were positioned and bring out the family—thirteen women and children in one room who had gone without food or water for over twenty-four hours.

The team replied that they were picking up sick and wounded from the neighborhood. The Marines warned them they would soon be going through to "clear the houses," with air strikes in support. "If you're going to do this you gotta do it soon."

Hurrying on to their initial destination nearby, they found a man face down in a white dishdasha, unarmed, shot in the back with his chest cavity blown out the front. The man's sons came out of their home, crying and shouting. The volunteers picked up the body and put it in the back of the truck. Until then, none of the dead man's family dared leave the house, which forced them to violate the tradition of immediately washing and preparing a corpse for burial. He was fifty-five, his sons said. A sick woman and two little girls came out of the dead man's house. Jo and Rana shielded the girls' heads so they wouldn't see the grisly cargo in the back, and helped the girls into the pickup.

Witnessing this, people poured out of houses, hoping to be escorted to safety, anxiously asking whether they could all leave, or just women and children. Jo related their questions to the Marines who responded that men of "fighting age" could not leave. When pressed, a Marine thought for a moment and ruled it meant anyone under forty-five, no lower limit. The rest, Jo wrote, "would be trapped in a city about to be destroyed . . . It's going to happen out of the view of the world, out of sight of the media, because most of the media in Fallujah is embedded with the Marines or turned away at the outskirts." Before they could pass on the bad news, however, two explosions scattered all the residents back into their homes and Rana left with the pickup for the medical clinic.

As Jo waited nervously in no man's land for Rana to return, the families hid behind their walls. She could see Marines watching them through binoculars. At this most unlikely time, this young woman who came to Iraq as part of a small troupe of clowns intending to entertain street kids, pulled out her disappearing hanky.

There was method to her madness, she explained. "I'm sitting like a lemon, nowhere to go, gunfire and explosions aplenty all around, I make the hanky disappear, reappear, disappear. It's always best, I think, to seem completely unthreatening and completely unconcerned, so no one worries about you enough to shoot."

The volunteers shuttled more women and children to relative safety and the dead to the morgue, but then the time came for the bus and an ambulance to return to Baghdad with the wounded. When Rana announced she intended to stay and help, Jo and Dave quickly agreed. But Ghareeb, their guide into Fallujah, warned he didn't have contacts with every group of resistance fighters, only some. With the wounded needing to get to Baghdad quickly and civilians still hiding in their homes waiting to be evacuated, the team reluctantly agreed to board the bus, promising to return as soon as possible.

"I hate the fact that a qualified medic can't travel in the ambulance but I can," Jo wrote later, "just because I look like the sniper's sister or one of his mates, but that's the way it is today and the way it was yesterday and I feel like a traitor for leaving, but I can't see where I've got a choice."

Their return to Baghdad was fraught with close calls. At one point, the two vehicles got separated. For tense moments, Jo and the rest of the passengers on the bus were stopped by an armed group they didn't know. Eventually they were allowed to pass.

Before crossing into the American lines near Abu Ghraib, they swapped seats: foreigners with their head scarves off in the front, Iraqis at the back. The U.S. soldiers, happy to see Westerners, searched the men and let the bus pass.

At one U.S. checkpoint, with several Iraqi cars following their bus, Jo and Dave tried negotiating with the troops to allow more Iraqi men to leave with their families.

"They agreed to let through one man of fighting age per car as long as he was the driver and was with his family," Jo recalled. "We attempted to negotiate for more men to be let out because husbands and fathers, of course, wanted to stay with their families and many did not want to fight. The soldier, whose name I do not know, said 'We want to keep them all in there, we can kill them all more easily.'"

Back in Baghdad, the satellite news reported that George Bush sent an Easter greeting to U.S. troops, saying, "I know what we're doing in Iraq is right."

Into her journal Jo poured out her anguish and rage.

"Well George, I know too, now. I know what it looks like when you brutalise people so much that they've nothing left to lose. I know what it looks like when an operation is being done without anaesthetic because the hospitals are destroyed or under sniper fire and the city's under siege and aid isn't getting in properly. I know what it sounds like too. I know what it looks like when tracer bullets are passing your head, even though you're in an ambulance. I know what it looks like when a man's chest is no longer inside him and what it smells like and I know what it looks like when his wife and children pour out of his house.

It's a crime and it's a disgrace to us all."

CONCLUSION: LEAVING IRAQ

After two months in Iraq, sharing a family's supper in a farm village surrounded by razor wire, accompanying army troops on patrol in an APC, and watching a troupe of Brit clowns entertain kids in a refugee camp, all that was left was the twelve-hour drive to Amman, Jordan, for the flight back home.

Shortly after dawn, Faris, driver and translator one last day, as he has been for several weeks, knocked on room 412 of Baghdad's Agadir Hotel. Trained as an engineer and with the heart of a humanitarian, he was typically punctual and charming.

At the boisterous taxi terminal, travelers converged from every direction. The cabbies' advance men sang out to attract customers, "Amman, Amman . . . Mosul, Mosul . . . Syria . . . Basra . . . Najaf." This transport system's efficiency predated the Ba'athists and will outlive the Capitalists.

Faris bargained in Arabic one more time for his American friend. Familiar with scrapping a living in Baghdad, he was not about to let a cab driver or baggage handler beat him out of a single dinar. Knowing this about him, it was all the more impressive when his goodbye gesture was to refuse payment.

The previous day, what kind of vehicle to take across the border was the topic of some debate among my former roommates at the Agadir. SUVs are comfortable, but they're also the transportation of choice for foreign businessmen and mercenaries, making them ready targets for highwaymen and resistance fighters. During my time in Iraq, I carefully followed the common wisdom among independent journalists to never even ride in a new taxi. In line with that wisdom, I chose a sedan instead of an SUV.

The workhorse sedan for that grueling trip was typically an early '90s Chevy Caprice. Its rounded styling gave it the nickname, "dolphin." So for the grand sum of $35—which later that morning included a breakfast of cheese, flatbread, cookies, fresh mandarin oranges, and the ubiquitous chai—I rode the dolphin to Amman.

There was already one other passenger aboard, and the driver informed me that when the back seat was full we would leave—or we could pay an additional ten dollars each and leave immediately. It was too good a deal to pass up and in five minutes we were on our way.

The driver, Majid, was a small, wiry guy with short, salt-and-pepper hair. Isama, the front seat passenger, was the rare fat person I'd seen during my visit. I correctly guessed he was a Jordanian and surmised later by his numerous jokes that he was also a salesman.

As soon as we were underway, Majid turned on a tape of slow, sorrowful-sounding Muslim chants. In a minute, the Martyrs' Bridge carried us over the Tigris River and the familiar pattern of mosques and street scenes rolled by: a ten-story communications center, bombed and looted black; the former Information Ministry in similar shape; Saddam Hussein's uncompleted "world's largest" mosque; a furniture district's couches and chairs crowding the sidewalk; an elderly kafia-clad biker driving an even older sidecar motorcycle; an army convoy bristling with guns held by young soldiers finishing their last days in Iraq; and a scrap-metal cart pulled by a high-stepping red horse.

On the highway out of town that leads to the airport and then skirts Fallujah and Ramadi, an Abrams Tank lumbered alongside the road, snarling traffic. It escorted an Army foot patrol searching for IEDs. The median, once lush with mature date palms and underbrush, had been clear-cut to deny cover for resistance fighters. Roadside vendors finished setting up their stands. A single exit sign announced two destinations: the towns of White Gold Village and Abu Ghraib. The latter was home to Saddam Hussein's infamous prison, and now houses thousands of U.S. detainees. A man grazed a single cow in the median. Shepherds tended flocks in the fields as women hand-cut hay and hauled it in enormous sacks as large as they were. It was barely 8:00 A.M. as we left Baghdad, on our way to Jordan.

The dolphin's speedometer registered 70 mph, but then it only went up to 80. Did that mean we wouldn't be able to drive the standard 100 mph in the sparsely traveled desert reaches, or that we just wouldn't be able to know what speed we were going ? Dirt exit and entrance ramps added to the sense of remoteness. We passed grim heaps of twisted guardrails that had been ripped from their posts by Army bulldozers to reduce hiding places for IEDs. Along this stretch of highway, it was considered unusually calm when a day went by without a bomb blast.

"Mistah Mike! Breakfast?" Majid asked.

"Sure! Yes! Nam!" I replied hungrily.

"Later," he says, pointing farther down the road.

His attempts at conversation could only be described as valiant, given my almost complete lack of Arabic. After five tries I understood his simple question, "What kind of car do you have in Amerikee?" Undaunted by this difficult process, he pulled a photograph of his three children from under the sun visor and asked me if I have any of my own. I produced a photo of my daughter and me at an Ohio peace demonstration, days after U.S. bombs started falling on Baghdad a year ago. She held a sign that said "9/11/01: 15 Saudis, O Iraqis." Majid smiled and I longed to ask him what he thought of it, but Faris was many kilometers behind.

Waking from a quick nap, the passing scenery momentarily startled me. I could barely believe I was looking at the western Iraq desert! In two months this landscape had become familiar, but this was the first time I saw real beauty in it, instead of just feeling disoriented by its arid starkness.

One sign of rebuilding that wasn't here before was a long line of bright, shining electrical transmission towers that gleamed against the azure sky. I wanted to take a picture but stopping along that section of highway was not considered wise. A week earlier, I had prevailed on my cab driver to stop not far from that spot so I could photograph a pile of guard rails. When I got back in the car, Faris informed me I had nearly given him and the driver both a stroke.

"Later" and breakfast time arrived and we pulled into a tiny roadside establishment that appeared out of nowhere. Majid turned around to give me the drill.

"Mistah Mike—breakfast, welcome. WC, welcome." Then, he made a mouthing motion with his hand and admonished seriously, "No talk! No talk! OK? Amerikee—no talk!"

This time I got his drift immediately. We had just passed Fallujah and Ramadi, two hot spots of anti-American resistance, and nobody needed a blue-eyed Westerner walking around speaking English. I quickly picked a nationality, and because in a pinch I could muster ten words of Tex-Mex Spanish, I pointed to myself and told Majid with a wink, "Ramadi, Fallujah . . . Espana sahife (journalist)." Both he and Isama laughed and breathed a sigh of relief.

After taking breakfast in the dolphin, we were back on the highway. Majid again turned to me and at something over 80 mph took both hands off the wheel to draw an imaginary line across the palm of his left hand with his right index finger. Pointing back and forth several times to either side of the line, he gesticulated "way" down the road and said, "Soldiers." Indicating way down the road again, he repeated, "Soldiers . . . Amerikee. Soldiers . . . Amerikee. You talk."

By then I had a good enough idea of what was going on to know that Majid had found a useful role for his Amerikee passenger when we hit the border—and I was confident enough with our level of communication to pull his chain.

"Espana! Espana sahife," I deadpanned, pointing to myself.

"Espana?" He replied, with a very confused look. "Espana? No—Amerikee. Amerikee sahife!"

I couldn't resist messing with Majid's mind one more time. "Amerikee?? No! Espana . . . Espana sahife!"

"Amerikee . . . soldiers . . . you talk," he responded, looking almost desperate. And then he got the joke.

Before we reached the border, it was time for a pit stop at the most godforsaken filling station on the planet where I got one more lesson in how to be a useful passenger.

Majid and Isama busied themselves rearranging luggage in the dolphin's trunk, eventually pulling out several cartons of cigarettes. First Isama and then Majid tried giving me a couple of cartons.

"La sucran (no thank you) . . . la smoke."

They said something else in Arabic and extended the cigarettes again. I refused politely. Puzzled at this extremely generous custom, I returned to the back seat. My fellow travelers talked for a while longer at the trunk and then it dawned on me what they were probably saying: "How many times do you think we'll have to explain to that idiot how to help smuggle cigarettes across the border?"

At the border lineup, with "my" two cartons of cigarettes sitting atop my bags, Majid gave me a final lesson in Useful Passenger 101. Tapping his shoulder to indicate an army officer's rank, he said, "Amerikee sahife . . . airplane . . . Amman . . . 8," and pointed to his watch.

So this American journalist had a flight out of Amman at 8:00 P.M. and couldn't be fooling around with typical border formalities . . . it sounded like a reasonable way to reduce the expected three-hour crossing fiasco. How much it would cost for this "express service" was a question I figured we'd deal with later. It turned out I didn't have to worry because the Iraqi officer I pitched that line to shot me a look that said, "Yeah, sure. You and every other western geek that's come through here today."

In due time, we paid for our exit visas, (since "transit" travelers like me— people staying in the country less than twenty-four hours—are not supposed to be charged this fee, I hoped the $10 I paid the sergeant would go into his kids' college fund) got our passports stamped, and were ready to complete the trip to Amman. But not before one more incident of cigarette smuggling.

After negotiating Jordanian customs but before we hit the road again, a man approached Majid's car window and pulled two cartons of cigarettes out of his overcoat. They engaged in an animated conversation that twice nearly ended with the stranger walking away in disgust. But eventually they reached an agreement, the stranger placed his cigarettes in a black plastic bag, taped it securely, labeled it, and passed it through the window to our driver. A couple of hours into Jordan at a desert café, we stopped for a late lunch. As Majid paid his bill, he handed his carefully wrapped contraband to the clerk working the cash register, exchanged a few words, and went on his way. In an hour or so, the owner of the illegal smokes would pick them up from the same clerk and the operation would be successfully completed.

Reaching Amman, Majid deposited me at an informal taxi terminal on the edge of town where he hugged me goodbye and I returned his bootlegged cigarettes. Grateful for this part of the journey to be completed, I was then faced with negotiating a ride to my two-star hotel. First the drivers wanted to take me to much nicer establishments, run by brothers and uncles. When that failed, they demanded nearly as much to take me across town as Majid charged to cross the desert. I'm not the greatest bargainer, but goodnaturedly I turned down their offers until the price was halved and agreed to that. No doubt Faris would still be appalled but I felt slightly victorious.

AFTERWORD: WHERE ARE THEY NOW?

After each trip to Iraq, I responded to numerous requests for presentations. At each, people were very engaged, asking questions and commenting about our involvement in the war and what they had learned about the people of Iraq. The most common observation, expressed in almost "Eureka"-like fashion was, "These people are just like us!"

"Well, what did you expect? I haven't just returned from Mars," is what I wanted to say, but kept in mind that the Bush administration and his allies in the corporate news media had done a remarkably successful job demonizing Saddam Hussein and ignoring the other 24 million inhabitants of Iraq.

So I took this comment as a positive sign and followed it into a discussion on the fundamental, simple fact that yes, these people are indeed just like us. Gradually, I appreciated this humble realization as one of the most important insights I had brought back from Iraq. If *Inside the Red Zone* is the least bit successful, it will remind others that Iraqis are indeed just like us.

Here is what has happened to some of the Iraqis and some of the Westerners since we met.

Zuhair Al-Jezairy

Nearing sixty, this journalist's journalist left his post as assistant managing editor of *Al-Mada* in mid-2005 after some disagreements with the owner. He said that such problems have been known to happen in other papers, when papers are owned by political parties or individuals with political interests. "Journalist feel more free and independent from the political agenda," he wrote, always the diplomat.

When I interviewed him in early 2004, he told me *Al-Mada*'s daily circulation was usually around 10,000. Almost two years later, it had slipped to about 4,000, although it still had offices and distribution in Basra, Mosul, Arbeel, and Sulaymania. In an e-mail message, Zuhair explained the reason for the circulation decline as one familiar to U.S. newspapers. His country's twenty-eight TV stations ". . . start to play greater role in Iraq than the written media (with) more interest in the entertainment programs."

Still, counting dailies, weeklies, and monthlies, Iraq has 180 newspapers as of mid-2005, with *Al-Mada* one of 10 dailies. The major Baghdad dailies and their circulations are: *Al-Sabah,* owned by the government, 10,000 to 15,000; *Al-Zaman,* 5,000 to 10,000; *Al-Sabah Al-Jedeed,* 8,000; and *Al-Masriq,* 8,000.

Not surprisingly, he said major issues in the dailies have been the elections and the new constitution, along with ongoing coverage of "the two main things, the terror and corruption . . . Today it is the next election and the terror and corruption. We are following also the government campaign to soften the tension between Sunni and Shiaa."

He believes his fellow citizens have "started to catch the political process . . . I think most of the Iraqis are going to the election. The Iraqi security forces will be ready in the next 2 years to hold the security and the American should put an agenda for Withdrawl. But at the same time the car Bombs will continue for other years."

Mr. al-Jezairy is currently working on a video documentary.

Voices in the Wilderness (Voices)

The suitcases of over-the-counter medicines I took to Iraq in February 2003 represented a tiny fraction of what some seventy Voices delegations, over seven years, took to Iraq in purposeful violation of the U.S./U.N. economic sanctions.

At the beginning of 1996, Voices members made it clear in a letter to U.S. Attorney General, Janet Reno, that they intended to break the sanctions law on conscientious grounds. The group's letter cited a U.N. Food and Agriculture Organization report that stated that "as many as 576,000 children have died as a result of sanctions imposed against Iraq by the United Nations Security Council," and cited estimates by UNICEF officers that another 1.5 million children would "eventually suffer malnutrition or a variety of unchecked illnesses because the sanctions make antibiotics and other standard medicines impossible to get."

Voices also invited Reno, "in your capacity as guardian of justice in the United States, and in your concern for children who are the primary victims of the embargo, to join us in demanding that the U.S. government lift this embargo, which in its real effects is immoral and unjust." Not surprisingly the Attorney General did not respond to the invitation but, within a week, the Treasury Department's Office of Foreign Asset Control (OFAC) wrote to warn Voices they were risking criminal penalties of up to 12 years in prison and $1 million in fines, plus civil penalties of up to $250,000 per violation.

Undeterred, Voices responded to the OFAC enforcement officer they were aware of the potential penalties, thanked him "for the clarity of the warning," and advised him that ". . . we will continue our effort to feed and care for the children and families of Iraq. We will do so by collecting medical relief supplies and then by openly and publicly transporting these supplies into Iraq for delivery to people in need."

Voices delegations continued traveling to Iraq for nearly three more years before OFAC issued a "pre-penalty notice" informing the peace group of its intent to levy a $120,000 penalty against the organization and $43,000 in fines against several individuals charged with violating the sanctions by taking medical supplies and toys with them to Iraq.

Via letter and a news conference at the National Press Club, the peace group made it clear to the Treasury Department it would comply neither with the sanctions nor with the government's requirement for a license to take humanitarian supplies to Iraq. As Kathy Kelly said, "It is a human right to take food and medicine to fellow human beings when they are suffering. No one should ever need a license for that." Defiantly, Voices refused to pay the fine and pledged to deliver $120,000 more in medicines to Iraq.

The federal government eventually levied a $20,000 fine on the group and set a June 24, 2004 hearing in U.S. District Court in Washington, DC.

Voices' response to the announcement of a trial date was to counter-sue the U.S. government ". . . for reparations for the Iraqi people due to the catastrophic effects of 14 years of US led economic sanctions . . ." and stating it would continue to ". . . nonviolently resist all payments, fines, taxes, and laws that perpetuate war and restrict our rights and responsibilities as world citizens."

On August 12, 2005, Federal District Judge, John Bates, ordered Voices to pay the $20,000 fine. In a press statement issued from their Chicago office two days later, the group was unrepentant.

"Voices will not pay a penny of this fine," the statement said. "We choose to continue our non-cooperation with the government's war on the Iraqi people through the simple act of refusing to pay this fine. To pay the fine would be to collaborate with the U.S. government's ongoing war against Iraq. We will not collaborate."

Since then, Voices has gone out of business. Having always traveled lightly, without even the burden of incorporation papers, it didn't take long for volunteers to close out the meager bank account and disappear. Additional volunteers, attracted by the group's principled defiance of the government, joined several Voices veterans to form a new group, Voices for Creative Nonviolence, drawing up a new round of activity:

- In over ninety cities across the United States, the United Kingdom, Ireland, and Switzerland, activists participated in the "100,000 Rings Campaign," that took place over October 24–28, 2005, to mark the anniversary of the release of a study in the British medical journal Lancet which calculated that 100,000 Iraqi civilians had been killed in the U.S. invasion and its immediate aftermath. In each city, organizers pledged to ring a bell 1,000 times, intoning the name of an Iraqi who had been killed in the war.
- The "Wheels of Justice Tour" bus continues to crisscross the country, taking literature and speakers about the occupations in Iraq and Palestine to dozens of cities and towns.
- Three Voices members plan on going to Syria for intensive studies in Arabic.
- The "Winter of Our Discontent," a combination of demonstrations, civil disobedience actions, and a month-long fast, is scheduled for mid-February through mid-March, 2006 to mark the third anniversary of the U.S. invasion of Iraq.

Faris

This electrical engineer-turned translator/driver/fixer with a big heart and cynical wit has concentrated on making a living and helping support his mother, working at what is available in the shattered Baghdad economy.

We keep in touch by email and I look forward to his frank reflections about the new Iraq and his personal role in it, such as the following excerpts he gave permission to include here.

After I have stopped working for the good guys—the NGOs, journalists, and peace activists—I joined the bad ones, meaning the military, the Coalition Provisional Authority and Companies. I had been working for people using civilized and peaceful ways to implement their believes then moved to the aggressive ones using weapons to let the Iraqi nation dreams come true.

It was very easy for me working for the first part but not the same way with the second one especially when many of the Iraqi nation dreams came true with their help. Toppling Sadams regime, the elections, the constitution and the hole continuing political process are all achieved by force to serve democracy and freedom for Iraq.

Sure, there is no doubt that all what has been achieved in Iraq from toppling Sadams regime, the constitution, the elections and the political process are all done by force. Otherwise, what all the military in Iraq has been doing here? Having a vacation or something?

As much as I believe all what has been done for Iraq is great, the controversy of achieving it using all that much violence and weapons arise the doubts inside me weather how long these achievements will stay and resist not being changed to what was before during Sadams era. The collation has to guard their achievement forever in this country because there is not enough Iraqi mentality that is correspondingly going with them. Building any structure on the ground can be done by force but no way into the mind.

This nation needs the good guys whom use civilized ways in order to achieve their believes to show them the way not forcing them into it.

It (using civilized ways) will not be as easy as what has been significantly done, but more resistant to be changed in case any dictatorship like Sadam might come where there are a lot of them not only in Iraq but every where I guess. Continuity is a very important factor to be taking care of here but who cares? If some political party will bite his share, let the flood eat the rest of Iraq.

Raping Iraq has been done by the assistant of many Iraqi political parties. If a dog bite a peace of meat, it will not care about the other hungry dogs. These political parties has bite its share of Iraq quary, they don't care a shit about the poor Iraqis whom have no big teeth. Sorry for my mistake that I made — political parties similar to dogs, actually they below dogs.

The time will take the Iraqi nation to achieve their dreams of democracy and freedom using the civilized ways will be longer than the time took the US military to do it by force and it will be more reliable for the future not to return back to the old dictatorship eras. What has been done in Iraq went without improving the Iraqi mentality towards what democracy and freedom really mean and how they should be hence, what has been achieved is very fragile and can be gone easily if the US military will not guard it in Iraq till the last drop of oil here.

Eventually, it is the Iraqi nation chalange. Many people has been cheated before but a lot of them are realizing what is going on now. The rest of them will realize one day, it is just a matter of time and pain.

In December 2005, he wrote to say he proposed to a lovely young woman in his city. I assume from the photos he sent that her answer was "Yes."

Christian Peacemaker Teams (CPT)

On April 28, 2004, CBS News' *60 Minutes* program broadcast the first of many now-infamous photos of prisoners being abused in Abu Ghraib. Less than a week later, Seymour Hersh's landmark article on that same subject appeared in the *New Yorker* magazine. What few people know is that months before the *New Yorker* and *60 Minutes* stories, the CPT in Baghdad had compiled a detailed report on seventy-two cases of alleged abuse of Iraqis by the U.S. military.

The very next day after his *New Yorker* article hit the newsstands, Hersh appeared as a guest on National Public Radio's *Diane Rhem* show. Peggy Gish, a CPT team member back home in Athens, Ohio after several months in Baghdad, called to tell him what she and her CPT colleagues had learned about abuse in the U.S.-run Iraqi prisons. Hersh spoke with her and later with Gene Stoltzfus, a CPT coordinator living in western Ontario.

Stoltzfus recalled that reporters were "greatly interested in pictures, but we didn't have pictures. The part we were able to play was to tell them 'You're on the right track. Keep digging.' And we were able to refer reporters to specific individuals because we had developed relationships. When the Abu Ghraib story blew up, the team in Baghdad and I were deluged with calls from the press. Some days, I'd spend almost 12 hours on the phone with reporters."

The 66-year-old Canadian said he'd learned from his time as a civilian in Vietnam during that war that, "When you're in a situation like what Iraq became, you try to document everything that comes along carefully, don't overstate it . . . because even a level-headed story will blow the top off what people think what's going on."

He said when he met with the CPT team in Baghdad in the fall of 2003 as they began compiling their report on abuses committed by the U.S. military, he stressed, "This is going to be a big mess—the misuse of power, the interrogations, the belittling of human life that always goes on in war."

"The best a group like CPT can do is to isolate a piece of the story and try to tell it. It may take us ten times or twenty-five times, but the story will eventually get out. We don't know when it's going to happen, but it will," he added.

Reflecting on what has transpired as a result of the revelations of torture and abuse in Iraq, Stoltzfus concluded, "It's very clear to me that the (Bush) administration, in response to the news from Abu Ghraib, has basically developed a new human rights policy that says it's OK to beat people—a setback to the policy that's been developed over the last 60 years, and not one that the American people blindly support, either."

On November 26, 2005, four members of the CPT in Baghdad were taken hostage by a previously unknown Iraqi resistance group, "The Sword of Righteousness." Jim Loney, one of the CPTers with whom I spent several days in early 2004, was one of those captured. Here is an article I wrote on them that appeared on several Internet sites December 8, 2005.

Not Even to Save Our Lives

> On a Thanksgiving visit home two years ago to his family in Sault Ste. Marie, Ontario, Jim Loney tried to explain to his father why he wanted to go to Iraq with Christian Peacemaker Teams. He told his Dad about a grade school chum, Rick, sent to Afghanistan with the Canadian Armed Forces, who narrowly escaped death from a roadside bomb.
>
> "If Rick was being asked to risk his life as a soldier then I, as a pacifist Christian who believes that war is not the way to peace, should be prepared to take the same risks," he recalled trying to reason with his father.
>
> Jim returned from Iraq safely, but on a return trip this year, his father's worst fears were realized. On November 26, Jim was taken hostage in Baghdad, along with three CPT colleagues, Harmeet Sooden, also from Canada, Norman Kember, from England, and Tom Fox, from the U.S.
>
> Millions of people around the world are learning for the first time about these peace warriors. But what few people know is that CPT members go to conflict zones like Iraq expressly stating that if they are abducted they do not want to be rescued by the military or any violent means.
>
> Claire Evans, delegate coordinator in the organization's Chicago office, read the following from the CPT's "Team Statement" adopted by each team going into a conflict situation. "We reject the use of violent force to save our lives in the event

we are kidnapped, held hostage or caught in the middle of a violent conflict situation. We also reject violence to punish anyone who has harmed us."

Gene Stoltzfus, a retired CPT coordinator, explained why the group's members go out of their way to renounce violence even to save their own lives. "We are a nonviolent group. We can't preach nonviolent action in protection of human beings and then ask it to be used on our behalf . . . that would be inconsistent, inappropriate and incoherent."

Alluding to the organization's larger strategy, the retiree who volunteered as a civilian aid worker in Viet Nam in the mid-60's explained, "If we would be rescued by a military or police action and people were killed, it would set a precedent setting back the work we do."

He explained that CPT members, working in the nonviolence tradition and philosophy, are prepared to accept whatever happens as a result of their actions, all of which "becomes useful as a moral witness to point to the larger goal we're working for — a fair and just society."

"We would not have had the modern civil rights movement if people said, 'it's too dangerous to go across that bridge (the Edmund Pettis Bridge, in Selma, Alabama).' Danger is inherent in the nature of nonviolence."

The organization is not relying on the fates to rescue the four held in Baghdad, however. Family members of the hostages have thanked the Canadian government for its efforts, CPT has appealed to its considerable network of Sunni and Shia clerics across Iraq, appeals have been sent out in Arabic from CPT supporters in Palestine, and already over 200 prayer vigils and demonstrations for their release have been held on three continents, according to the CPT website.

True to CPT's principles, the catchphrase, "Love your Enemies; End the Occupation; Release the Peacemakers," has been appearing on banners at prayer vigils around the world, such as those at over a dozen churches in Italy last Sunday where the following prayer was said: "We pray for their kidnappers, that they may realize that violence will not help us build a better world. We pray for our four friends, that their faith may sustain them in these difficult times and that they may bear witness of the Christian love for one's enemies, as they have always done in their activity in support of the victims of war. We pray for all the Iraqis who have disappeared or are being held captive, that they may soon be reunited with their loved ones."

Yesterday, across Canada, CBC radio listeners heard an announcer play the haunting second movement from Henryk Gorecki's Symphony of Sorrowful Songs, offering it "as a public prayer" for the four hostages.

Two years ago on that holiday trip home, Jim Loney was not very successful explaining why he wanted to go to Iraq. His father's response to him at the time, quoted in an article Jim wrote was, "What can you accomplish by going there? It's futile. Every westerner is a target. They don't care who you are or why you're there. It's just not worth it."

Two days ago, Jim's family wrote the following, indicating his work is having an effect beyond Iraq, all the way to Ontario. "Our family would like to express its deepest gratitude for the tremendous support we have received from every corner of the world and from people of all faiths, especially the Muslim community. We know that our James would be overwhelmed by the grassroots support that he is receiving. We are too. We have come to a fuller understanding of the effect that his humanitarian work for peace has in the world."

On March 10, 2006, the body of Tom Fox, the only U.S. citizen among the four CPT hostages, was found in Baghdad. On March 23, the remaining three hostages, Canadians Jim Loney and Harmeet Sooden, and Briton Norman Kember, were freed.

Dahr Jamail

The Alaskan mountain-climbing-guide-turned-independent-journalist returned to Iraq for several months in April, 2004 and again in November, 2004. In April, he covered the first U.S. siege of Fallujah, described in the chapter "Springtime in Fallujah." He returned to Baghdad the day after the 2004 U.S. presidential election, just as George W. Bush launched the second siege of Fallujah.

Lasting over a month, that battle displaced nearly all of the city's 300,000 residents. Dahr provided most of the unembedded reporting from the West, interviewing refugee eyewitnesses who poured into Baghdad and towns, villages, and open camps scattered outside Fallujah. At the end of the siege, the U.S. military allowed an Iraqi doctor access to Fallujah's streets to photograph some of the dead. Dahr obtained dozens of those graphic photos, posting them on his website for the world to see.

His interviews with refugees of the siege also provided details of a number of war crimes committed by the U.S. military, including running over the wounded in the streets with tanks, shooting civilians holding white flags, firing on ambulances, and the use of white phosphorus as a weapon. The abuses became so pervasive that Dahr began calling Fallujah "America's Guernica," a reference to the first city whose civilian population was bombed from the air, when Nazi planes struck it during the Spanish Civil War. Just as the CPT's documentation of prisoner abuse at Abu Ghraib was ignored by corporate news media outlets for several months, nearly a year would pass before "serious" news agencies picked up the story about white phosphorus being used as a weapon in Fallujah. To date, little, if anything, has been published in the mainstream press on the other crimes Dahr reported from Fallujah's refugees.

In addition to his singular coverage of Fallujah, Dahr completed extensive reports on the state of the Iraqi water system and Bechtel Corporation's job rebuilding it, the condition of hospitals in major cities in Iraq, and the plight of Iraqis displaced internally by the war. With no plans to return in the immediate future, he nonetheless continues to write on conditions based on information he gets from sources living in Iraq, providing some of the only western news reports and photos of U.S. military operations like "Steel Curtain" in western Iraq. He now lives in California and has yet to visit his cousins in Lebanon.

Jo Wilding

The combination bubble-blowing clown who entertained Iraqi kids in squatter camps around Baghdad and heroic activist who rescued civilians under fire in Fallujah moved back to southern England where she is raising her new son and attending law school, specializing in human rights.

In late 2005, she wrote to solicit contributions for another "Circus2Iraq" trip—this time to Palestine because of the danger of returning to Iraq.

Jo explained that one of her circus colleagues, Jenny, "spent quite a bit of time in Palestine and talked about teaching some kids to juggle using stones. It was the first time the children had seen stones as toys instead of weapons. As we saw in Iraq, play can transform objects, places and situations and we hope to do that again in Palestine. There are a lot of emotional problems among Palestinian kids because of the trauma they see. Like the children in Iraq, when given paper and pencils, they tend to draw tanks, guns and bombs. In Iraq we found that after a show they started drawing clowns, jugglers and magicians."

4th Infantry Division

One of the soldiers I accompanied on patrol during my visit to FOB Paliwoda turned out to be from a suburb of Toledo and I caught up with him eighteen months after he returned. Former Army Sergeant Brad Contat now teaches fifth-grade science and social studies, and said life is going well for his wife and two young daughters. He loves his job and the stability of his life after the military.

"It's also nice to use my experience as a veteran to talk with the students," the twenty-year-old said. "Like this last Veterans' Day, I was able to make a speech . . . to let the students know that what we do is all about them and freedom and that it's now up to them to carry the torch."

Contat served his three-year enlistment, including a year in Iraq, and is still eligible to be called up to active duty for the remainder of an eight-year obligation. Asked if he would go back if called, he hesitated briefly and said, "Well, I wouldn't want to go, even though part of me will always be there with the other guys who are still there. Would I go? Yeah, I would, but I wouldn't be too happy about it, now that I'm back with my wife and kids. I sure wouldn't want to put them through that again."

He said he has made the readjustment to civilian life "pretty well . . . I felt a little isolated at first, people not really understanding what you went through . . . and when I first got back I was having trouble sitting still, because you're always ready to go at a minute's notice over there, and a little trouble getting reacquainted with my family and finding a job. It was stressful for sure. But I have a great support system with my wife and family and I'm doing a lot better now with a fulltime job and being with my kids."

I reached Sergeant Contat's buddy, Staff Sergeant Adam Tymensky, on his cell phone at a Sears, Roebuck Company store in Michigan, where he and his wife, his 5-year-old daughter, and 2-year-old son had just taken their 2005 Christmas photo. His son was born during his first tour of duty in Iraq. The 29-year-old father was leaving for a second tour within the week.

In the Army since he was eighteen, Tymensky said he knew the United States would be in Iraq "for a while. I might have one or two more deployments. I signed up for this mission and will do it to the fullest of my capability. I'm dedicated to my job." His MOS (Military Occupation

Specialty) is "Scout," but he said, like all men and women in the infantry, his first job consists of keeping sharp in basic combat skills.

I asked him if he had been able to talk directly with any civilians the last time he was in Iraq. He said yes he had, but then explained that those times consisted chiefly of accompanying a senior officer to meetings where the officer had a translator and the Sergeant got by "with a lot of sign language and pointing."

Susan Galleymore

The "Uncommon Mom," who traveled halfway around the globe to visit her son stationed with the Army north of Baghdad, has seen her relationship with him become strained. In late 2005, she wrote to let me know the latest between them, what her son is doing now, and what she has planned for her "MotherSpeak" project.

> Nick and I communicated somewhat after my trip to Iraq. Then, I communicated with him when I was in Crawford, Texas supporting Cindy Sheehan's effort at Camp Casey. He appeared unhappy that I was there. I wasn't able to hear Nick clearly (because of the reception) but he hung up on me when I explained what I was doing there: waiting to hear from the president what noble cause our kids and Iraqis and Afghans are dying for. Since then (August) I've called him and left messages for him several times but we've not communicated directly.
>
> Actually, what is interesting is that I told Nick before he deployed to Iraq that, if anything happened to him, if he was wounded or killed, that I would dog Bush, Cheney, Rummy, Condi, and Colin . . . that they would know my son's name and what had happened to him because of their trumped up war . . . and that I would dog them even after they were out of the White House. At that time, Nick told me I was indulging my personal little drama. Since Cindy Sheehan appears to feel exactly as I would have and is acting similarly to how I would have acted, I've not heard what my son thinks of the public drama accompanying Cindy's vigils.
>
> I can say that this is both painful on an immediate level and also scares the hell out of me if I allow myself to project how life might be if he continues this silence into the future. I know that he communicates with his father who, last time I talked to him, believed and approved of Bush's (many and varied) rationalizations for The War on Terror.
>
> I want to say that, when I have talked to Nick, prior to Camp Casey (when my presence there clearly indicated my sentiments) I never try to persuade him to my point of view. My work with MotherSpeak is my public work, my conversations — minimal as they are — with my son are personal and I do not express anything that I think might confuse his first task: staying alive and as uninjured as possible through this war.
>
> I have visited wounded troops in Walter Reed (Army Hospital) and, Mike, I never want to see my kid there. I don't want to see other mothers' kids there either . . . it is a horror and a nightmare to see and listen to those people try to make sense of their futures with the wounds they have.

He is now a fully fledged Special Forces medic. He begins his Arabic language training in January and it continues for six months. At that time he'll be eligible for re-deployment. It is amazing that he has accomplished so much and successfully completed such vigorous training. And, it is not a co-incidence that he has chosen to be a medic. I believe Nick sincerely wants to do good things and serve his countrymen . . . as do so many other young, idealistic Americans. The travesty of these times is the cynical betrayal of these young people by the Bush administration, the Congress, and our national leaders.

"MotherSpeak" leaves for Israel and Palestine on Monday Nov 28, 2005. I'll be interviewing a cross-section of people there, both Israeli and Palestinian and sharing their stories about war and terror. MotherSpeak continues small steps towards developing and presenting a system's view of war and terror by sharing stories of families affected by war and terror. MotherSpeak is dedicated to the belief that the more we know about how we civilians are all implicated in militarism, the more fiercely we will work to prevent the next war.

Next May I hope to travel to Russia to interview mothers from Committee of Soldiers' Mothers. These women don't even bother to work through the Russian government but go directly onto Russian military bases to retrieve their sons abused by the Russian military. They are also reaching out directly to Chechen mothers to end that war and terror. You go, moms!!

Baghdad College High School Students (BCHS)

I was able to reach a couple of the BCHS students who participated in the letter exchange with students in Toledo. Unfortunately, neither of them had heard back from the U.S. students they wrote to, but here is a glimpse at what their lives are like today.

Fahad is now in his first year of medical school at Baghdad University. He writes, "about the situation in Iraq its really hard the security now is in the lowest level not only because of the terrorists and also because of the government they r doing nothing but stealing our money the problem is that they r not working for iraq they r working only for themselves and for other countries especially for Iran which is (in my opinion) the most dangerous country for Iraq coz they r trying to spread their islamic revolution to iraq which is not fit for a country like iraq because of its various ethenic groups."

He added that the economy is "really bad the government raised the prices of fuel in Iraq 3 times than before, (and dont ask me about the electrisity if u know what I mean)."

The email I sent to Amjed found him at his new home in Canada. He wrote that he "still contact(s) my friends back in Iraq. Your letter brought back nice memories of my school."

He is in the twelfth grade and "planning to apply for life or health sciences. It is hard and needs a lot of efforts to become successful here. I have two jobs. I work at a fast food restaurant and I tutor math, physics, and chemistry. I am also a member of the chess club, newspaper club, and soccer team in my school."

In response to my question if I should wish him Happy Eid, or Merry Christmas, he replied, "Eid Mubarak or Christmas? They are both joy and signifying happiness. I wish you a beautiful, wonderful, and successful new year."

And So Many Others

As for Sheik Alawa, Shalon, Mohammed, Yaseen's uncle, or the other people living behind the wire in Abu Hishma, or the eighty-plus men and boys rounded up in the middle of the night in the devastated hamlet of Abu Siffa, or the women missing husbands and brothers in the village of Al-Jazeera, or Pila or Hamis from the She La squatter's camp—who knows? More to the point: who cares? They are the common people of Iraq whose towns and villages make the news only when targeted for a brand name military operation such as Steel Curtain, Just Cause, or Iron Hammer.

These are the people who, on the rare occasion when they are named, have the devilish term "fog of war" associated with their story, as in: "The fog of war prevents Mohammed's family from finding out where he was taken by U.S. troops . . ." or "the fog of war makes it impossible to say just how Mrs. Taha's brothers were killed." They are the ones who, when the U.S. news media records their deaths following an air strike in Al-Anbar province, are listed among the "suspected terrorists" whose deaths we are supposed to rejoice.

If courageous activist groups like Voices and CPT, or independent journalists like Dahr Jamail didn't risk their lives and spend their own money venturing to meet these people and tell their stories, we would likely never hear of them. Indeed, Kathy Kelly's explanation of how the U.S. government successfully whipped up support for an invasion of Iraq pretty much says it all. "We are not told anything, really, about the 24 million people who live in Iraq. We are only told how terrible Saddam Hussein is, and we are left with the impression he is the only person living in Iraq."

The rich, the politically connected, and the powerful who live and work in the Green Zone, have no problem getting their stories heard. It's the people in the Red Zone who do the suffering and the dying whom we need to know more about. Mainstream journalists with expense accounts and adequate resources need to talk with more of these truly heroic people; not just to fill a "detainee story" quota, but with the respect due to people who can teach us much about maintaining human dignity in hellish conditions—something Americans experience only rarely as in the aftermath of natural disasters. The very least the common folk of Iraq deserve is to have their stories heard.

We need to hear them as much for our own sake as for theirs. For until we open our ears and our hearts to their stories we will never be able to answer the larger questions, such as what do we owe Iraq and its people? What will the peace movement demand of the U.S. government? Has this war made us more safe or less? Having enforced brutal sanctions and carried out intermittent

Samar Hassan, 5, screams after her parents were killed by U.S. Soldiers with the 25th Infantry Division in a shooting January 18, 2005 in Tal Afar, Iraq. The troops fired on the Hassan family car when it unwittingly approached them during a dusk patrol in the tense northern Iraqi town. Parents Hussein and Camila Hassan were killed instantly, and a son Racan, 11, was seriously wounded in the abdomen. Racan, paralyzed from the waist down, was treated later in the U.S. (*Photo by Chris Hondros/Getty Images*)

bombings for a dozen years *before* invading in 2003; having reduced whole cities to rubble; having killed over 100,000 people, maimed many thousands more, and laid waste to Iraq's environment; having lain its entire economy prostrate to international corporations; what now? Do we allow our government to claim "we gave them democracy" and call it a day? Do we replace U.S. ground troops with U.S. bombers and Marines "over the horizon" as some in Congress urge and call that a withdrawal? Having killed over 2,500 U.S. soldiers and maimed well over ten times that number, will we force the government to remember the veterans of this war long after the politicians are done using them as election campaign props? Having spent hundreds of billions of dollars to control the resources in a strategic corner of the world, will citizens of what claims to be the world's greatest democracy find the collective will to turn our government from empire to the real needs of people?

To anyone with even a modest sense of history, these questions will sound familiar. They are essentially the same unanswered questions that have allowed the Vietnam War and its aftermath to fester in the body politic for two generations. We do the same with Iraq at the peril of generations unborn.

INDEX

About the Author

MIKE FERNER is an American peace activist, a member of Veterans For Peace, and a freelance journalist who has published articles and commentaries on Iraq and other current affairs issues in such periodicals or online venues as the *Nation, Truthout, Z, Common Dreams,* and *Counterpunch.*